The Jewish Genealogical Society of Great Britain
Registered Charity No. 1022738

A BEGINNER'S GUIDE
TO JEWISH GENEALOGY
IN GREAT BRITAIN

Edited by Rosemary Wenzerul
Chairman
Education Committee

זכר ימות עולם בינו שנות דר-ודר
שאל אביך ויגדך זקניך ויאמרו-לך :

Remember the days of old, consider the years of many generations:
Ask thy father, and he will declare unto thee: Thine elders, and they will tell thee.
Deuteronomy XXX11 v.7   דברים לב ז

Published by
The Jewish Genealogical Society of Great Britain
Registered Charity No. 1022738
PO Box 13288, London, N3 3WD.
email: jgsgb@ort.org
website: www.ort.org/jgsgb

Printed by
The Printing Place Ltd
☎ 01245 251001

ISBN 0-9537669-0-X

Front cover designed by
Rosemary Hoffman and Derek Wenzerul

**Copyright © 2000
The Jewish Genealogical Society of Great Britain**

At the time of printing the information contained in the Guide is accurate however, information can become out-of-date. This Guide is sold, therefore, on the condition that neither the Authors of each section nor the Society can be held legally responsible for the consequences of any errors or omissions there may be.

CONTENTS

FOREWORD
Rosemary Wenzerul

'A Beginner's Guide to Jewish Genealogy in Great Britain' is the first of a new series of booklets to be published by The Jewish Genealogical Society of Great Britain. It was designed specifically for the beginner in genealogy but will also be useful for those who need inspiration to continue their research. Whether you are, a teenager or a senior citizen, Jewish or not this Guide will not only show you **what** to do but **how** to make use of what you find.

Members of the Society have written each section. We have tried to take you step by step through the process of tracing your own family history by explaining, as simply as possible, the various stages of research available to you. We have endeavoured to make this Guide into a reference document with as many addresses as possible throughout the British Isles and have included a small address section for research abroad.

Genealogy is a very popular and fast growing pastime. Whilst increased accessibility of both computers and the Internet have made many more resources available to everyone, there is still no substitute for visiting archives and looking at records.

We hope this Guide will give you an insight into the world of Jewish genealogy and encourage you to do further research in the future.

I would like to take the opportunity of thanking the following members of the Education Committee and the Society for their help and commitment in producing the Guide: George Anticoni, David Fielker, Bella Fox, Cyril Fox, Peter Glass, Maurice Hoffman, Rosemary Hoffman, Saul Issroff, Joe Ross and Derek Wenzerul. In addition, I would particularly like to thank David Fielker for his editorial advice and Derek Wenzerul for all his help with the technical side of producing the Guide.

Rosemary Wenzerul
Chairman, Education Committee
Member of Council

January 2000

INTRODUCTION
George Anticoni

Congratulations. You have taken the first step in an exciting and engrossing adventure and entered the world of Genealogy. Please remember that we all had to begin somewhere. We all took those first faltering steps into our ancestors' past. Most of us had little or no knowledge when we started - whatever level of expertise some of us may since have gained.

It really does not matter how long the journey into your ancestral past takes you. Time is on your side. Work at your own pace. Many of us lead busy lives and will have to fit genealogy into our life schedule. You can work at it, leave it for a while, return to it as you wish to and are able to. You are under no pressure where genealogy is concerned. What is time to a genealogist?

In this Beginner's Guide we have tried to cover the basic stages and trust that the information it contains will be of assistance to you when beginning your own family research.

Should you decide to become a member of The Jewish Genealogical Society of Great Britain (JGSGB) you will receive our Journal - *Shemot* - and our *Newsletter*. Both of these are packed with interesting items.

Members are invited to join us in our activities (details below); visit our library **(see map on page 33)**. We will always be pleased to meet you personally and our Council members are always ready to help.

JGSGB - SPECIAL INTEREST GROUPS (SIGs):
For details see under section entitled 'Going Further Afield (Europe and Elsewhere)'.
JGSGB FAMILY HISTORY WORKSHOPS:
These workshops are an excellent opportunity for beginners to find out how to trace their family. There is a panel of JGSGB experts available to answer your questions. Workshops take place on a number of Sunday afternoons throughout the year, as published in the JGSGB's programme and *Newsletter*. The normal venue is the Sternberg Centre, 80 East End Road, Finchley, London, N3 2SY **(see map on page 36).**
MONTHLY MEETINGS:
These are usually held at Finchley Synagogue **(see map on page 33)**. Dates and times are given in our *Newsletter.*
ANNUAL SEMINAR:
A full days programme of lectures on Jewish genealogy usually held on a Sunday in November. Full details are given in our *Newsletter.*
George Anticoni
Chairman, The Jewish Genealogical Society of Great Britain

HOW TO RECORD ORAL HISTORY
Rosemary Wenzerul

WHERE TO START:
Every member of the family has a story to tell, whether it be of their earliest memories; school days; achievements; career; engagement; marriage; honeymoon; divorce; family or friends. Perhaps they were in the Forces and on active service or a Prisoner of War (POW). However, it is essential at all times to respect the feelings of your interviewee who may not always wish to recall various parts of their lives.

VARIOUS METHODS OF RECORDING YOUR INTERVIEW:
It is important that the reminiscences of relatives should be collected and preserved for future generations to enjoy and cherish.

There are three ways of doing this:

1 **AUDIO:**
   By recording their recollections on tape.
   The purchase of a small battery/mains powered tape recorder with a separate microphone or one that has the facility for one to be plugged in is advisable. Check to see if it also has a counter, as this will assist you in finding specific sections of an interview and is useful when you come to indexing. I would mention that one hour of taped interview could take as long as 10 hours to transcribe!

2 **VIDEO:**
   By recording their memories on video.
   A video camera makes an interview more interesting. It will enable you to capture the mood and emotions of the person you are interviewing. At a later date, with this method, it is possible to add music, titles and even still photographs.

3 **WRITTEN:**
   By taking notes during the interview.

DECIDE WHO TO INTERVIEW FIRST:
Once you have decided the manner in which you wish to carry out your interview, decide which member of the family you would like to interview first. It would be more sensible to start with the oldest member of your family. Contact them and set a time and a date. It is very important to try to develop a rapport with them. The art of a good interview is getting someone to talk in a relaxed and informal manner. This is particularly the case with the older generation who may be concerned about having their conversation taped or on video. Remember to keep the interview as informal as possible. A useful tip is sometimes to interview two relatives together; as they tend to spark each other off!

PLAN YOUR INTERVIEW:

It is essential to plan your questions well in advance of your interview and to use a structured checklist (see page 8) and the 30 suggested questions (on pages 11/12) that contain the essential information you require from your interviewee. Open-ended questions will give better results e.g. 'Tell me about....', 'How do you....', or 'Describe for me...', etc.

Do make your questions clear and short and show an interest in what the person is saying. Be a good listener and try not to interrupt. It would be more sensible to make a note of any discrepancy you may have and ask for clarification after the interview otherwise you may miss out on further recollections that may have been forthcoming and of interest.

Try not to impose your views, as the interviewee may end up telling you what they think you would like to hear rather than what they really think. Sometimes looking through the family photograph album may inspire the interviewee to recollect old memories and stories about the persons concerned, perhaps how they lived their lives or where they came from, etc. It is vital to collect as many memories, however short they may be, from all your relatives. These recollections will bring your family history to life rather than just collecting pages and pages of dates and names.

If your relation mentions someone with a nickname or perhaps refers to someone as 'Papa', ensure you ask for his correct name and relationship.

You may wish to ask the person if they have any other memorabilia you could see. Do this at the end of the interview otherwise the person may decide to look for it during the interview and disrupt their train of thought.

Don't try to collect all the information you require at one interview. Allow about 1-2 hours for the interview. If you are interviewing an elderly person he/she may become tired and this may not produce the best results. You can always return another time to pick up where you left off.

TIPS ON MAKING A GOOD RECORDING:

1   Be familiar with your equipment.

2   Check you have all the equipment needed and that it is in good working order. Always take additional batteries and tapes.

3   Avoid background noises (e.g. radio, television, people talking, traffic noise).

4   Ensure the microphone is placed correctly (roughly 10-12" away from the interviewee's mouth). Should the microphone be placed too close to the tape recorder or you have the volume turned too high, you may pick up interference.

5   Having tape-recorded the interview, remember, if you wish to keep the recording, to break off the record tabs on your tapes after the interview so that they cannot accidentally be erased.

FAMILY CHECKLIST

PLEASE PRINT CLEARLY

YOURSELF	Your Name		Your Spouse's Name	
Please give full names	....		....	
Previous surname(s) where appropriate				
Date/Place **(birth)**	....		....	
Date/Place **(marriage)**	....		....	
Date/Place **(death/burial)**	....			
Occupation	....		....	
Your Children's names*	1..................	2..................	3..................	
Date/Place **(birth)**	1..................	2..................	3..................	
Date/Place **(marriage)**	1..................	2..................	3..................	
Name of spouse	1..................	2..................	3..................	
Their children*	1..................	....	....	
*(if more than 3 children	2..................	....	....	
use an extra sheet)	3..................	....	....	

YOUR PARENTS	Your father		Your mother (maiden name)	
	....		....	
Date/place **(birth)**	....		....	
Date/place **(marriage)**	....		....	
Date/place **(death/burial)**	....		....	
Occupation	....		....	
Your siblings	1..................	2..................	3..................	
Date/place **(birth)**	1..................	2..................	3..................	
Date/place **(marriage)**	1..................	2..................	3..................	
Name of spouse	1..................	2..................	3..................	
Occupation	....		....	
Their children*	1..................	....	....	
	2..................	....	....	

YOUR GRANDPARENTS	Paternal Grandparents		Maternal Grandparents	
Names	....	....	....	....
Date/place **(birth)**	....	....	....	....
Date/place **(marriage)**	....	....	....	....
Date/place **(death/burial)**	....	....	....	....
Occupation	....	....	....	....

Any other information..
....

LOOKING AFTER YOUR TAPES:

Should you wish to keep your tapes for many years, it is advisable to purchase good quality tapes. Cheap cassette tapes are not recommended for long-term storage as they may deteriorate in time. The life span of your tapes will also depend on whether they are exposed to excessive heat or damp. To avoid this they should be stored in their boxes in a cool and dry place.

INDEXING OF YOUR TAPES:

Indexes should contain basic information about the interviewee's life history. It is important to have a reference system, which provides a certain amount of personal detail about the interviewee. The easiest method of doing this is to give each person interviewed a number. It might be advisable to record in your index, which transcript pages refer to which side of the tape and to note the order in which the different sections of your questionnaire were asked. Note too any recollections or stories you feel were of particular interest.

COPYING AND RESTORATION OF OLD PHOTOGRAPHS:

Relatives who own old photograph albums may not want you to borrow them in case they are lost or damaged. It is, however, very easy to re-photograph old photographs in situ from an album. It is preferable to use a close focusing reflex camera immediately above the photograph album on a table and position the tripod/camera immediately above it so you can see exactly what you are taking. Use daylight (preferably north light) so the light is not directly onto the photo. If there is insufficient light, use a white piece of card, which will help to reflect the light onto the photograph. Use colour film as opposed to black and white film as it is cheaper and easier to process.

With regard to the restoration of old photographs: if you do not have access to a computer and are unable to scan the photographs yourself and the negatives have long disappeared, there are many professional photographic firms around who can digitally improve them with their computerised retouching system. They are able to remove the damaged areas, bring the colours back to life and restore them to their original quality. However, unless your photograph is really something special and warrants restoration, this is an extremely expensive service.

Perhaps you would like to turn your photograph into a gift!! There are firms who do a lovely selection of gifts which incorporate your own photograph e.g. table mats; coasters; canvas prints; mugs; jig-saws, T-shirts.

REMEMBER:

Remember to send your interviewee a copy of your transcript together with a note thanking them for their help and time.

FURTHER READING:

Humphries,S.   The Handbook of Oral History.
                                Inter-Action In print 1984.

Iredale,D. and Barrett,J.   Discovering your Family Tree.
                                Shire Publications Ltd.

Kurzweil,A.   From Generation to Generation.
                                Harper Perennial 1996.

McLaughlin,E.   First Steps in Family History.

Pelling,G.   Beginning your Family History.

ACKNOWLEDGEMENT:
I would like to thank Jolene (Knowles) Abrahams for allowing me to use some of her genealogical material. Jolene is a past President of the Livermore-Amador Genealogical Society and is Co-Regional Director for the California State Genealogical Alliance with her husband David.

30 SUGGESTED QUESTIONS
Rosemary Wenzerul

1 Has anyone in your family produced a family tree? If so who?

2 See 'Family Checklist' on page 8 for details required from the relative/s you are interviewing.

3 If your relative came from abroad, how did he/she travel to England?

4 What was the town you came from like?

5 Did your grandparents live in the same place?

6 What was your occupation/positions held?

7 How did you meet your spouse?

8 Tell me about your parents?

9 Tell me about your siblings?

10 What was your life like as a child (including the sweets you enjoyed; the games you played; your friends; clubs and organisations you belonged to, etc.)?

11 What were your   hobbies? Did you belong to the Guides, Scouts or Jewish Lads Brigade?

12 At what age did you leave school? Which school?

13 Describe your Mother's kitchen when you were a child?

14 Was your Father in the Forces? Do you have his regimental details or army record?

15 Was he on active service? If yes, where?

16 Do you have any interesting stories he told you about his time in the forces?

17 Do you own a family bible or prayer book?

18   Do you have any old photo albums?

19   Do you have copies of any birth, marriage/ketubot or death
        certificates?

20   Do you have any family stories or specific family phrases, which
        have been passed down to you?

21   What would you change if you could live your life again?

22   What diseases or conditions, if any, have affected your family?
        e.g. colour blindness, heart disease, diabetes.

23   Did you have holidays as a child/adult? Where did you go?

24   Was your family religious?

25   What Synagogue did you belong to? Get married in?

26   Do you have any family recipes, which have been handed down
        to you?

27   What are your happiest/unhappiest memories?

28   Have you kept any memorabilia?
        (e.g. valentine cards, birthday cards, anniversary cards; wedding,
        barmitzvah/batmitzvah party invitations; certificates; menus; membership
        cards).

29   What did you do during the War? Were you in the forces, land
        army, ARP or other?   Where were you stationed?

30   Were you evacuated? If so, what was it like? Where were you
        sent? What was the family you stayed with like? What school did you
        attend?

USING PUBLIC RECORDS
Rosemary Hoffman

This section is about beginning searches from British Public Records.

What are public records? They are records which are kept by government and other public bodies for all kinds of purposes; usually we think of our birth, marriage and death certificates, but there are also wills, electoral registers, census records, court records, some military records. Records such as membership lists of professional bodies may not be public, but the names of committee members could be and might include an ancestor's name.

How do I start? Unless you know there is an illustrious relative in the family with whom you claim relationship, you will work backwards.

If you have talked to members of your family, you may have some ideas on where to begin, but suppose you have little or no information.

Civil registration began in 1837 in England and Wales, 1855 in Scotland and 1864 in Ireland. However registration was not compulsory. Whilst it was necessary to go through the registration process before a burial took place, there was no incentive to register births. It was the Registrar who had the incentive through being paid on the number of Registrations of births, marriages and deaths. Compulsion to register came through the Births and Deaths Registration Act 1874, this Act tightened up procedures in England and Wales. The record for which you are looking may therefore not exist. For Jewish persons you may have to look for a burial record instead of a death registration.

Start with yourself. (If you know the names of your grandparents you could start your search further back). A full birth certificate gives date and place of birth, baby's forename(s) (if decided at time of registration), sex, father's name and occupation, mother's name and maiden name, and name address and description of the informant. A "short" certificate will show only the baby's forename(s) (if decided at time of registration), surname, sex and date of birth. Both of these forms of certificate will have an entry number to link back to the original registration.

Be warned: if the parents were not married or if the mother was a single parent the father may not be named.

If the parents are named and appear to be married the information can be used to trace their marriage certificate, and thence their parents' names.

The census was taken every 10 years since 1801, except in 1941. The census years of relevance to genealogists are 1841-1891. This is because the earlier censuses lack individual names and the later ones are secret for 100 years. The next census is due in 2001, when the information from the 1901 census should also be made available.

Once you can find someone who was alive in one of these census years you can start to use the census. A useful guide when you have your census returns is 'Making sense of the census' which tells you what all the little marks delineate.

Although searching the census might look daunting, remember that the population of Great Britain was considerably smaller in the 19th century. It was only 38 million in 1901 and only 20 million in 1851.

The 1881 census has been indexed by surname. A single address may consist of several households but lines across one of the columns show the demarcation between each household. All persons living at an address should have been included, together with their age, place of birth, occupation and relationship to the head of the household. The age given may not always be accurate; often people gave their wrong age or used a bit of poetic licence! Once you have found your ancestor on a census, it is well worth looking at the same address for 10 years earlier: you may find they stayed there. Alternatively you may find they were in the same neighbourhood or even in the same street. The useful thing about the census is that you now have the names and ages of all the siblings of a particular generation and you can start search for their births and so on, for each person on the list, provided they were in Great Britain. These can lead you to different addresses.

If you have a common name, you might need to get the certificates to confirm it is correct; if your name is sufficiently unusual you will not need to do this. You might find that some of the older siblings were born at a different address and this will then lead you to an earlier census.

For earlier censuses a map such as a reprint from Ordnance Survey maps will be useful. You may have to search whole neighbourhoods as each census used different districts. Look up the enumeration districts for the streets you are interested in and then go through the records.

Marriage records can be searched by the wife or husband's name; however after 1911 marriages are cross-referenced to spouses (useful if one of your names is too common). Having found the names that match, you can get the certificate. If you have two alternatives the records office can help you sort out which you want.

Death records can be searched in the same way. They may not be as accurate as any other record as it depends on the informant who may have had to guess at someone's age, for example. After 1969 the deaths indexes usually show date and place of birth.

Wills for England and Wales after 1858 are obtainable from The Principal Registry of the Family Division. For earlier wills the Family Records Centre has microfilm copies of the Principal Prerogative Court of Canterbury (PCC) for 1384-1858. This was the High Court for the southern half of the country. It has indexes of wills from 1858-1943. The northern counterpart was the Principal Prerogative Court of York (PCY).

Wills are useful in clarifying relationships. For example they might mention sons-in law or daughters-in-law or other in-laws you may not know about. If someone remarried there may be a will containing names you are unaware of, especially if the person had a new family. They can also contain details of possessions. You may read about an object or document which you know of or even possess.

Electoral registers are based on address. Universal suffrage has only been around since 1928 but some women over 30 could vote in 1918. Your local archive or history library might have copies of old electoral registers. In the early part of the century you only voted if you were a ratepayer.

The Public Record Office is a treasure house; when beginning genealogy the most useful records there are naturalisations (document classes HO1, HO144, HO 344) and forces records. It is necessary to plan visits carefully in advance so that you are aware of all relevant dates etc. Research at the PRO is fascinating, but can be very time consuming.

A reader's ticket is issued on the spot, on presentation of acceptable proof of identity documents. (Telephone in advance if in doubt).

Naturalisation records dating from the late 18th century until 1940 are available. You can see an individual's naturalisation papers. They contain person's application, various supporting statements, a police report, and sometimes records of payments to a friendly society that helped with the naturalisation. They also contain a copy of the person's oath of allegiance. There are details of the applicant's family, place of origin, parents' names and length of residence. These records contain a wealth of detail and a slice of social history: many of the occupations mentioned have disappeared. The place of origin can be located by using something like the Encarta atlas. However, you will find that the information changes with the date, the later the more information. The background papers are also secret for 75 years, though one can obtain access to them sometimes. (See section on further reading.)

The **RGS Map Room** Kensington Gore, London, SW7 **(see map on page 34)** has historical maps and gazetteers to help your search. (If names and countries have changed you will certainly have to do this.)

Did your ancestor serve in the forces? The PRO has records going back well into the 17th century but most Jewish people will be interested in records after 1850 or so. For the First World War you can find out what medals were awarded to each person. The PRO is currently undertaking a project to microfilm the records of all WW1 personnel and these are gradually being released. At the present time the only record available are of those who left the forces before the cessation of hostilities, i.e. they were invalided out.

It is worth looking at the WWI British Jewry Book of Honour, which is in the JGSGB's library **(see map on page 33)**.

For WWII the PRO has lists of aliens who were exempted from internment. Copies of the exemption certificates contain biographical details and the place of origin as well as their address (in the 1940's); there may also be some other records available.

Trade directories
If your ancestor had a trade or profession you may find their name in trade directories.

These are some of the ways you can begin to look at your family history. Obviously there are many other sources you can use to put more flesh on the bones. What I have tried to do here is to help new genealogists to start on their own family history. Of course, it is hoped you will really get hooked and delve deeper. Who knows what you can find out? Genealogy can be very rewarding but it can also be very time consuming. Happy searching!

Useful addresses: Please see under section entitled
                          'Jewish Genealogical Research in Great Britain'

Further reading:

Adler, M.   WW1 British Jewry Book of Honour.
                          (Available from the library of The Jewish Genealogical
                          Society of Great Britain).

Field, D.M.   Step by Step Guide to Tracing your Ancestors:
                          Reed Consumer Books, London, 1982. Useful guide to
                          Sources, addresses may not all be up to date.

Fielker, D.   Hounding the Home Office. *Shemot*, October 1994
                          Vol.2 No.4. (Journal of The Jewish Genealogical
                          Society of Great Britain).

Higgs, E.   Making Sense of the Census. London: HMSO,
                          1989.

Format of Birth Certificate

CERTIFIED COPY OF AN ENTRY OF BIRTH
GIVEN AT THE GENERAL REGISTER OFFICE, LONDON
Application Number _____

REGISTRATION DISTRICT

19 _____   BIRTH in the Sub-district of _____   in the _____

Columns:-	1	2	3	4	5	6	7	8	9	10*
No.	When and where born	Name, if any	Sex	Name and surname of father	Name, surname and maiden surname of mother	Occupation of father	Signature, description and residence of informant	When registered	Signature of registrar	Name entered after registration

CERTIFIED to be a true copy of an entry in the certified copy of a Register of Births in the District above mentioned.
Given at the GENERAL REGISTER OFFICE, LONDON, under the Seal of the said Office, the _____ day of _____ 19 ____

CAUTION:- It is an offence to falsify a certificate or to make or knowingly use a false certificate or a copy of a false certificate intending it to be accepted as genuine to the prejudice of any person or to possess a certificate knowing it to be false without lawful authority.

Format of Marriage Certificate

19 _____ Marriage solemnized at _____ in the _____

in the District of _____

REGISTRATION DISTRICT

Columns:-	1	2	3	4	5	6	7	8
No.	When married	Name and Surname	Age	Condition	Occupation	Residence at the time of marriage	Fathers name and surname	Occupation of father

Married in the _____ according to the usages of the _____ by _____

This marriage { } In the { }
was solemnized { } presence { }
between us { } of us { }

CERTIFIED to be a true copy of an entry in the certified copy of a register of Marriages in the Registration District of _____
Given at the GENERAL REGISTER OFFICE, under the Seal of the said Office, the _____ day of _____ 19___

This certificate is issued in pursuance of section 65 of the Marriage Act 1949. Sub-section 3 of that section provides that any certified copy of an entry purporting to be sealed or stamped with the seal of the General Register Office shall be received as evidence of the marriage to which it relates without any further or other proof of the entry, and no certified copy purporting to have been given in the said Office shall be of any force or effect unless it is sealed or stamped as aforesaid.

CAUTION:- It is an offence to falsify a certificate or to make or knowingly use a false certificate or a copy of a false certificate intending it to be accepted as genuine to the prejudice of any person or to possess a certificate knowing it to be false without lawful authority.

WARNING: THIS CERTIFICATE IS NOT EVIDENCE OF THE IDENTITY OF THE PERSON PRESENTING IT

Format of Death Certificate

CERTIFIED COPY OF AN ENTRY OF DEATH
GIVEN AT THE GENERAL REGISTER OFFICE, LONDON
Application Number _____

REGISTRATION DISTRICT _____

19____   DEATH in the Sub-district of _____ in the _____

No.	Columns:- 1 When and where died	2 Name and Surname	3 Sex	4 Age	5 Occupation	6 Cause of Death	7 Signature, description and residence of informant	8 When registered	9 Signature of registrar

CERTIFIED to be a true copy of an entry in the certified copy of a Register of Deaths in the District above mentioned.
Given at the GENERAL REGISTER OFFICE, under the Seal of the said Office, the _____ day of _____ 19____

CAUTION:- It is an offence to falsify a certificate or to make or knowingly use a false certificate or a copy of a false certificate intending it to be accepted as genuine to the prejudice of any person or to possess a certificate knowing it to be false without lawful authority.

19

JEWISH GENEALOGICAL RESEARCH IN GREAT BRITAIN
David Fielker

VITAL RECORDS (England & Wales)

ONS, The Family Records Centre, 1 Myddleton Street, London ECIR IUW
Tel: 020 8392 5300 - Fax: 020 8392 5307 **(see map on page 35)**
Web-site: http://www.open.gov.uk/pro/prohome.htm

Public search room has indexes to births, marriages and deaths, 1837 - present; arranged alphabetically by surname, by quarters (ending March, June, September, December) to 1983; from 1984, alphabetically by surname by year. Reference numbers in indexes necessary to order copies of certificates, (there is a charge for certificates), mailed within a few days.

Birth certificates give date, place, father, mother (incl. maiden name), father's occupation, name and address of informant.

Marriage certificates give date and place of marriage, names and ages of couple, occupations, addresses, names and occupations of fathers, witnesses.

Death certificates give date and place of death, name, age, occupation, cause of death, name and address and relationship of informant.

VITAL RECORDS (Scotland)

General Register Office for Scotland,
New Register House, Edinburgh, EH1 3YT, Scotland.
Tel: 0131 314 4446 - Fax: 0131 314 4400
E-mail: nrh.gros@gtnet.gov.uk
Web-site: <http://www.open.gov.uk/gros/groshome.html>
From 1855; computerised index; certificates on microfiches.

VITAL RECORDS (Northern Ireland)

Northern Ireland Registrar General, Oxford House, 49-55 Chichester St, Belfast, BT1 4HL
Tel: 028 9025 2010

Public Record Office, 66 Balmoral Avenue, Belfast, BT9 6NY
Tel: 028 9025 1318 - Fax: 028 9025 5999
E-mail: proni@nics.gov.uk
Web-site: <http://proni.nics.gov.uk/index.htm>

MARRIAGE APPLICATIONS (London's East End)

Tower Hamlets Local History Archives,
277 Bancroft Road, London, E1 4DQ.
Tel: 020 8980 4366 extn. 129 - Fax: 020 8983 4510
Marriage notice books for Stepney from 1926 and Bethnal Green 1837-1878 and 1920-1965 contain marriage applications, giving date, names of couple, marital status, profession, age, address, length of residence in UK, place of intended marriage.
(The library also has a wealth of material on London's East End, local newspapers from 1857, censuses and electoral registers).

ANNOUNCEMENTS

Jewish Chronicle Library, 25 Furnival Street, London, EC4A 1JT.
Tel: 020 7415 1500
Web-site: www.jchron.co.uk
Volumes of back issues. Useful for birth, marriage and death announcements and obituaries. Card index of names appearing in titles of articles. Appointment necessary.

or contact:

Dr. & Mrs. A.P. Joseph,
25 Westbourne Road, Edgbaston, Birmingham. B15 3TX.
Tel: 0121 454 0408 - Fax: 0121 454 9758
(Full set on microfilm of Jewish Chronicles from 1841).

WILLS AND ADMINISTRATIONS

Principal Registry of the Family Division,
1st Avenue House, 42-49 High Holborn,
London, W1V 6NP.
Tel: 020 7936 6000 and 020 7936 6801
(Records were previously held at Somerset House)
From 1858, England and Wales. Arranged alphabetically by surname, annually.
Family Record Centre, 1 Myddleton Street, London, EC1R 1UW.
(see map on page 35).
Microfilm copies of the Principal Prerogative Court of Canterbury for 1384-1858

CENSUS RECORDS

Family Records Centre, London, see above. See also Tower Hamlets Library above.
1841, 1851, 1861, 1871, 1881, 1891.
Address necessary; no index to names. Lists all residents by name, age, relationship to head of household, place of birth (district in UK, otherwise country).

The 1881 census is available on CD-ROM from the Church of the Latter Day Saints (see section on Mormons for more details). 1881 has an index on microfiche at the Family Records Centre. 1851 is indexed for the Whitechapel area.

NATURALISATION RECORDS

Public Record Office, Ruskin Avenue, Kew, Surrey. TW9 4DU.
Tel: 020 8876 3444 - Fax: 020 8878 8905 **(see map on page 36)**
Web-site: http://www.open.gov.uk/pro/prohome.htm
Indexes under surnames (document class HO1) indicate surname, first name, naturalisation date and place, country of origin, and cover 1844-1900, 1901-1910, 1911-1914, 1915-1924, 1925-1930, 1931-1935. Staff will explain how to order the original certificates and the 'background papers'. Certificates (document class HO 334) give name, address, occupation, place and date of birth, nationality, marital status, first name of wife, names and nationality of parents (not usually mother's maiden name). Background papers (document class HO144) include the application. Early ones (to around 1900) give date and place of birth, parents, names and ages of children, residences in UK; middle ones (around 1920s) add wife's name, date and place of marriage, details of education and occupation, full police report; later ones (1930s) can add details of siblings and education or occupation before arrival. Availability seems to vary.

INTERNMENTS

Many Jews were interned as aliens during the two world wars. Some records are at the Public Record Office.

OLD TELEPHONE DIRECTORIES

British Telecom Archives, 3rd Floor, Holborn Telephone Exchange,
268-270 High Holborn, London, WC1V 7EE.
Tel: 020 7492 8792 (help desk) - Fax: 020 7242 1967
E-mail: hayda@boat.bt.com **(see map on page 33)**

Post Office Archives and Record Centre,
Freeling House, Phoenix Place, Mount Pleasant Complex, London, EC1A 1BB.
Tel: 020 7239 2570 - Fax: 020 7239 2576

ELECTORAL REGISTERS

In main public library in each borough, but not always complete. Also at the London Metropolitan Archives **(see pages 24,35)**. A complete present day set for the UK is at the Family Record Centre. Under addresses, lists of those eligible to vote: 1884-1918 - men only; from 1918 - women over 30 if householders or wives of householders, all men over 21; from 1928 - all over 21; from 1940s - all over 18.

SHIPPING RECORDS

Public Record Office, Ruskin Avenue, Kew, Surrey, TW9 4DU.
Tel: 020 8876 3444   **(see map on page 36)**
Web-site: http://www.pro.gov.uk/
These are in document classes BT26 (inwards i.e. arriving passengers), BT27 (outwards i.e. departing passengers). Class BT32 lists the ships that arrived and departed from each port. The passenger lists are arranged by British port from 1890, under name of ship, and only to and from places outside Europe. Information given for arriving passengers can include name, age, occupation, proposed address in Britain and the date of entry, but often had just surname. As these records are very bulky and lack an index, search time is lengthy and the resultant information is not always useful.

SYNAGOGUE RECORDS

United Synagogue, Beth Din
735 High Road, Finchley, London, N12 OUS.
Tel: 020 8343 8989 - Fax: 020 8343 6262
E-mail: us@brijnet.org;
Web site: www.brijnet.org/us/

Federation of Synagogues
65 Watford Way, NW4.
Tel: 020 8202 2263 - Fax: 020 8203 0610
General inquiries may take time, and there is usually a fee.

Sephardi Burial Society
2 Ashworth Road, Maida Vale, London, W9 1JY.
Tel: 020 7289 2573

Reform Synagogues of Great Britain
The Sternberg Centre for Judaism, 80 East End Road, London N3 2SY.
Tel: 020 8349 4731- Fax: 020 8343 0901
E-mail: admin@refsyn.org.uk **(see map on page 36)**

Union of Liberal & Progressive Synagogues
21 Maple Street, London W1P 6DS.
Tel: 020 7580 1663 - Fax: 020 7436 4148
E-mail: montagu@ulps.org

West End Great Synagogue
32 Great Cumberland Place, London W1H 7DJ.
Tel: 020 7724 8121 - Fax: 020 7723 4413

Assembly of Masorti Synagogues
1097 Finchley Road, London NW11 0PU.
Tel: 020 8201 8772 - Fax: 020 8201 8917
E-mail masorti.uk@ort.org

Union of Orthodox Hebrew Congregations
Adath Yisroel Synagogue, 40 Queen Elizabeth Walk, London, N16 OHH.
Tel: 020 8802 6226 or 020 8802 6262

LONDON METROPOLITAN ARCHIVES
40 Northampton Road, London, EC1R OHB.
Tel: 020 7332 3820 - Fax: 020 7833 9136 **(see map on page 35)**
E-mail: lma@ms.corpoflondon.gov.uk
Some minute books and members' lists, but letter of permission needed from Synagogue authorities to view. (The Archives also has electoral registers for most of London, hospital and school records, a good library, and a collection of old maps of London). The LMA also has some Jewish Free School records, which are not restricted.

INSTITUTE OF HERALDIC AND GENEALOGICAL STUDIES
Northgate, Canterbury, CT1 1BA.
Tel: 01227 768664 - Fax: 01227 765617
E-mail: ihgs@ihgs.ac.uk

ADDRESSES AND MAPS
Rosemary Wenzerul

LIBRARIES

LONDON

The British Library

96 Euston Road, London, NW1 2DB	Tel: 020 7412 7332
	Fax: 020 7412 7268
Map Library, London, WC1B 3DG	Tel: 020 7412 7702
Preservation Office, WC1B 3DG	Tel: 020 7412 7612
Official Publications, WC1B 3DG	Tel: 020 7412 7536
Philatelic Collections, WC1B 3DG	Tel: 020 7412 7635
Photographic Service, WC1B 3DH	Tel: 020 7412 7614
Reading Room (Enquiries) WC1B 3DH	Tel: 020 7412 7676
Admissions WC1B 3DH	Tel: 020 7412 7677
Book Reservations, WC1B 3DH	Tel: 020 7412 7667
24hr Book Ordering, WC1B 3DH	Tel: 020 7323 7683

(Great Russell Street, London, WC1B 3DH)
Electoral Registers are available at the British Library.
(Reader's ticket required for access to library)

The British Library Newspaper Library
Colindale Avenue, London, NW9 5HE. **(see map on page 34)**
Tel: 020 7412 7353 (to reserve volumes/microfilm
24 hours in advance) - Fax: 020 7412 7379
Web site: http://www.bl.uk/collections/newspaper
(18 years or over, identification necessary, last admittance 4.00 pm)
Jewish Chronicle, Jewish World and many other Jewish newspapers are available
in the Library both within the UK and abroad.

Family History Centre
Church of the Latter Day Saints, Hyde Park Family History
Centre, 64-68 Exhibition Road, London SW7 2PA.
Tel: 020 7589 8561 **(see map on page 34)**
International Genealogical Index (IGI)

Guildhall Library
Aldermanbury, London, EC2P 2EJ.
Tel: 020 7332 1868 - Fax: 020 7600 3384
Web-site: www.cityoflondon.gov.uk/search-guildhall

Holborn Family History Library
32-38 Theobalds Road, London, WC1X 8PA.
Tel: 020 7413 6342 (Main Library: 020 7413 6345) - Fax: 020 7413 6284

Huguenot Library
University College, Gower Street, London, WC1E 6BT.
Tel: 020 7380 7094 (by appointment only)
E-mail: s.massil@ucl.ac.uk

Institute of Jewish Studies
Jews' College Library,
Schaller House, 44a Albert Road, London, NW4 2SJ.
Tel: 020 8203 6427 - Fax: 020 8203 6420
E-mail: Jewscoll@clusl.ulcc.ac.uk
(There is a charge for using the library)

The Jewish Genealogical Society of Great Britain Library
Finchley Synagogue, Kinloss Gardens, **(see map on page 33)**
Finchley, London, N3 2SY
E-mail: JGSGB@ORT.ORG
Web-site: http://www.ort.org/jgsgb
Opening times: Please see the JGSGB *Newsletter*.
Jewish Genealogical People Finder, Avotaynu and many other UK and
overseas journals. Full library list see web-site above.

University College
Jewish Studies Library
University College, Gower Street, London, WC1E 6BT.
Tel: 020 7387 7050 - Fax: 020 7380 7373
The library of the Jewish Historical Society of England, Mocatta Library,
Brodie Library, Altman Library, Abramsky Library and William Margulies Yiddish
Library. Open to the general public for research by arrangement - I.D. required.

Wiener Library
4 Devonshire Street, London, W1N 2BH.
Tel: 020 7636 7247 - Fax: 020 7436 6428
E-Mail: lib@wl.u-net.com
Allows a free browse (especially welcomes JGSGB members)

SELECT LIST OF HISTORY LIBRARIES
AND ARCHIVE CENTRES

Lambeth Archives Department
Minet Library, 52 Knatchbull Road, London, SE5 9QY.
Tel: 020 7926 6076 - Fax: 020 7926 6080

Newham Local History Library
Stratford Reference Library, Water Lane,
London, E15 4NJ.
Tel: 020 8557 8856

Redbridge Central Library
(Local History Section),
Clements Road, Ilford, Essex. IGI IEA.
Tel: 020 8478 7145

Romford Central Reference Library
St. Edwards Way, Romford, Essex. RM1 3AR.
Tel: 01708 772389 - Fax: 01708 772391

Southwark Local Studies Library
211 Borough High Street, London, SE1 1JA.
Tel: 020 7403 3507 - Fax: 020 7403 8633

Valence Road Reference Library
Becontree Avenue, Dagenham, Essex. RM8 3HT.
Tel: 020 8592 6537 - Fax: 020 8592 5297

REGIONAL

Birmingham
Central Library & Archives
Chamberlain Square, Birmingham, B3 3HQ.
Tel: 0121 303 4220 - Fax: 0121 233 4458

Brighton
Brighton Reference Library, Church Street, Brighton, BN1 1UE.
Tel: 01273 296969 - Fax: 01273 296965

Bristol
Bristol Reference Library, College Green, Bristol. BS1 5TL.
Tel: 0117 9037 202 - Fax: 0117 9037 216

Manchester
Manchester Local Studies Unit, Central Library,
St. Peter's Square, Manchester, M2 5PD.
Tel: 0161 234 1979 - Fax: 0161 234 1963

Oxford
Bodleian Library
University of Oxford, Broad Street, Oxford, OX1 3BG.
(Contact Admissions office in advance of visit)
Tel: 01865 277000 - Fax: 01865 277182
E-mail: enquiries@bodley.ox.ac.uk

Leopold Muller Memorial Library
Oxford Centre for Hebrew and Jewish Studies
Yarnton Manor, Yarnton, Oxfordshire. OX5 1PY.
Tel: 01865 375079 (BY APPOINTMENT)
About 7 miles west of Oxford, just off A40 road. Contains the Kressel Collection, a biographical and historical archive covering over 12,000 Jewish personalities and the early Zionist period. In addition to which, a collection of Jewish books and Yizkor books.

Northampton
Northampton Central Reference Library
Abington Street, Northampton, NN1 2BA.
Tel: 01604 462040 - Fax: 01604 462055

Southampton
Hartley Library, Archives and Manuscript Department,
Hartley Library, University of Southampton,
Highfield, Southampton. SO17 1BJ.
Tel: 023 8059 2180 - Fax: 023 8059 5451
E-mail: library@soton.ac.uk

Suffolk
Suffolk Local Studies Library and Record Office
77 Raingate Street, Bury St. Edmunds, Suffolk. IP33 2AR.
Tel: 01284 352352/55 - Fax: 01284 352355

Walsall
Walsall Local History Centre and Library
Essex Street, Walsall. WS2 7AS.
Tel: 01922 721305 - Fax: 01922 634954
Web-site: http://www.earl.org.uk/earl/members/walsall

SCOTLAND
Edinburgh
National Library of Scotland
George IV Bridge, Edinburgh, EH1 1EW.
Tel: 0131 226 4531 - Fax: 0131 622 4803

Glasgow
The Mitchell Library, North Street, Glasgow, G3 7DN.
Tel: 0141 287 2999 - Fax: 0141 287 2815

WALES
Aberystwyth
National Library of Wales, Aberystwyth, Ceredigion, SY23 3U.
Tel: 01970 632811 - Fax: 01970 632852
E-mail: unedadcyf@llgc.org.uk

IRELAND

Dublin
Genealogical Office, National Library of Ireland,
2 Kildare Street, Dublin, 2.
Tel: 00-353-1 603 0200 - Fax: 00-353-1 676 6690

ARCHIVES

Cambridge Archive Service
Shire Hall, Castle Street, Cambridge, CB3 OAP.
Tel: 01223 717281 - Fax: 01223 717201

Dublin City Archives
City Assembly House,
58 South William Street, Dublin, 2.
Tel: 01 677 5877 - Fax: 01 677 5954

Hackney Archives
43 De Beauvoir Road, London, N1 5SQ.
Tel: 020 7241 2886
Web-site: http://www.hackney.gov.uk

Liverpool
Wirral Archive Service, Central Library,
Borough Road, Birkenhead, Merseyside, L41 2XB.
Tel: 0151 652 6106 - Fax: 0151 653 7320

London
London Metropolitan Archives (**see p.24 for address/p.35 for map)**

Scottish Jewish Archive Centre
Garnethill Synagogue, 127 Hill Street,
Glasgow, G3 6UB.
Tel: 0141 332 4911 BY APPOINTMENT

Sheffield Archives
52 Shorham Street, Sheffield, Yorks. S1 4SP.
Tel: 0114 273 4756 - Fax: 0114 273 5066

Southampton Archive Service
Civic Centre, Southampton, SO14 7LY.
Tel: 023 8083 2251 - Fa x: 023 8083 2156

Tower Hamlets Local History Archives
277 Bancroft Road, London, E1 4DQ.
Tel: 020 8980 4366 - Fax: 020 8983 4510

City of Westminster Archives
10 St. Ann's Street, London, SW1P 2XR.
Tel: 020 7641 2180 - Fax: 020 7641 2179

York City Archives
Art Gallery Building, Exhibition Square,
York, YO1 2EW.
Tel: 01904 551 879

PUBLIC RECORD OFFICES
For London see under section 'Jewish Genealogical Research in Great Britain'
Belfast
General Register Office
Oxford House, 49-55 Chichester Street,
Belfast, BT1 4HL.
Tel: 028 9025 2000 - Fax: 028 9025 2044

Bristol
Bristol Record Office
'B' Bond Warehouse, Smeaton Road, Bristol, BS1 6XN.
Tel: 0117 922 5692 - Fax: 0117 922 4236

Manchester
Greater Manchester County Record Office,
56 Marshall Street, New Cross, Manchester, M4 5FU.
Tel: 0161 832 5284 - Fax: 0161 839 3808

Northampton Record Office
Wootton Hall Park, Northampton, NN4 8BQ.
Tel: 01604 762129 - Fax: 01604 767562

Plymouth and West Devon
Plymouth and West Devon Record Office,
3 Clare Place, Coxside, Plymouth, PL4 OJW.
Tel: 01752 305940

SOCIETY OF GENEALOGISTS
14 Charterhouse Buildings, Goswell Road,
London, EC1M 7BA.   **(see map on page 35)**
Tel: 020 7251 8799 - Fax: 020 7250 1800
E-mail: info@sog.org.uk
Isobel Mordy Collection, Hyamson Collection, Colyer-Ferguson Collection, IGI Index

ROYAL GEOGRAPHICAL SOCIETY
Map Room, Kensington Gore, London SW7 2AR
Tel: 020 7591 3040 - Fax: 020 7591 3001
E-mail: library@rgs.org **(see map on page 34)**

SYNAGOGUE RECORDS
See under section
'Jewish Genealogical Research in Great Britain'

Bevis Marks Synagogue
2 Heneage Lane, London, EC3A 5DQ
Tel: 020 7626 1274
(Records of Births, Marriages and Deaths are published for sale)

Sandys Row Synagogue
Middlesex Street, London, E1 7HW
Tel: 020 7377 5854 (Caretaker)
Tel: 020 7375 0517 (Minister)

BOARD OF DEPUTIES OF BRITISH JEWS
5th Floor, Commonwealth House,
1-19 New Oxford Street, London, WC1A 1NF.
Central Enquiry Desk/Help Line:
Tel: 020 7543 5400 or 02017 543 5421/22 - Fax: 020 7543 0010

JEWISH HISTORICAL SOCIETY OF ENGLAND
33 Seymour Place, London, W1H 6AT
Tel/Fax: 020 7723 5852

BOOKSHOPS
Jewish Memorial Council Bookshop/Council
25 Enford Street, London, W1H 2DD.
Tel: 020 7724 7778 - Fax: 020 7706 1710
E-mail: Jmcbookshop@btinternet.com/Jmcouncil@btinternet.com

Manor House Books
John Trotter Books, Sternberg Centre,
80 East End Road, Finchley, London, N.3.
Tel: 020 8349 9484 - Fax: 020 8346 7430   **(see map on page 36)**
E-mail: jt@jt.demon.co.uk

MUSEUMS
Imperial War Museum
Lambeth Road, London, SE1 6HZ
Tel: 020 7416 5342 - Fax: 020 7416 5374
E-mail: books@iwm.org.uk

The Jewish Museum
Raymond Burton House, 129-131 Albert Street,
London, NW1 7NB.   **(See map on page 36)**
Tel: 020 7284 1997 - Fax: 020 7267 9008

The London Museum of Jewish Life
The Sternberg Centre, 80 East End Road, London, N3 2SY.
Tel: 020 8346 2288/020 8349 1143 **(see map on page 36)**

Museum of London
150 London Wall, London, EC2Y 5HN
Tel: 020 7600 3699 - Fax: 020 7600 1058

Manchester Jewish Museum
190 Cheetham Road, Manchester, M8 8LW.
Tel: 0161 834 9879/823 7353

National Army Museum
Royal Hospital Road, London, SW3 4HT
Tel: 020 7730 0717 - Fax: 020 7823 6573
E-mail: nam@enterpirse.nt
Web-site: http://www.failte.com/ngm/

Police Museums
West Midlands Police Museum, Sparkhill Police Station, 639 Stratford Road, Birmingham, B11 4EA. Tel: 0121 626 7181 - Fax: 0121 626 7066
Greater Manchester Police Force Museum, Newton Street, Manchester, M1 1ES. Tel: 0161 856 3287 - Fax: 0161 856 3286
Aliens were required to register with the police, and give details of birth place, address, date of birth, particulars of family etc., WWII enemy alien slips at the Public Record Office are only for aliens who were not interned. Some local records are available in Police Museums as above.

Royal Air Force Museum
Graham Park Way, Hendon, London, NW9 5LL
Tel: 020 8205 2266

Royal Naval Museum
H.M. Naval Base (PP66), Portsmouth, PO1 3NU.
Tel: 023 9272 7562 - Fax: 023 9272 7575

FREEMASONS

Library and Museum of the United Grand Lodge of England, Freemasons' Hall, Great Queen Street, London, WC2B 5AZ
Tel: 020 7831 9811

ASSOCIATION OF JEWISH EX-SERVICE MEN AND WOMEN (AJEX)
Jewish Military Museum and Memorial Room,
AJEX House, 5A East Bank Stamford Hill, London, N16 5RT
Tel: 020 8800 2844 - Fax: 020 8880 1117

COMMONWEALTH WAR GRAVES COMMISSION
2 Marlow Road, Maidenhead, Berkshire, SL6 7DX.
Tel: 01628 634221 - Fax: 01628 771208
E-mail: cwgc@dial.pipex.com
Web-site: www.cwgc.org
(War Records: See WWI British Jewry Book of Honour by Michael Adler
in The Jewish Genealogical Society of Great Britain (JGSGB) library)

British Telecom Archives (BT)
High Holborn, London, WC1

© British Telecom Archives

The Jewish Genealogical Society of Great Britain Library
Finchley Synagogue, Kinloss Gardens, London, N3 2SY

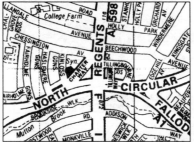

*Reproduced by permission of Geographers' A-Z Map Co. Ltd.
Licence No. B0210. This map is based upon Ordnance Survey maps
with the permission of the Controller of Her Majesty's Stationery Office*
© *Crown Copyright 1999*

Royal Geographical Society (RGS)
Kensington Gore, London, SW7
Mormon Family History Centre (LDS)
Exhibition Road, London, SW7

British Library Newspaper Library
Colindale Avenue, London, NW9

Family Records Centre
1 Myddleton Street, London, EC1
London Metropolitan Archives
40 Northampton Road, London, EC1
Society of Genealogists
14 Charterhouse Buildings, Goswell Road, London, EC1

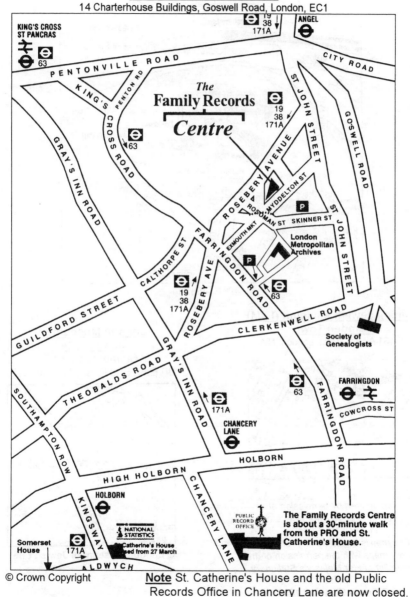

© Crown Copyright

Note St. Catherine's House and the old Public Records Office in Chancery Lane are now closed.

35

Public Records Office - Kew
Ruskin Avenue, Kew

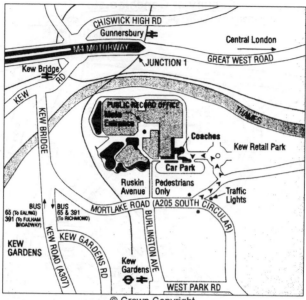

© Crown Copyright

London Jewish Museum (LJM)
Camden Town
129-131 Albert Street, London, NW1

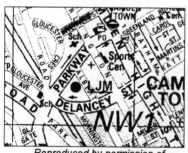

Reproduced by permission of
Geographers' A-Z Map Co. Ltd.
Licence No. B0210
This map is based upon Ordnance
Survey maps with the permission of the
Controller of Her Majesty's Stationery
Office.
© Crown Copyright 1999

London Museum of
Jewish Life
Sternberg Centre
80 East End Road, London, N3

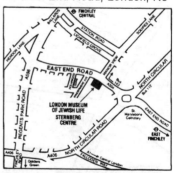

© **London Museum of Jewish Life**

MORMON FAMILY HISTORY CENTRES
Rosemary Wenzerul

The Church of the Latter Day Saints (LDS)(Mormons) Family History Centres (FHC) has a number of Centres throughout the United Kingdom where films of the various indexes may be seen. **The main Family History Centre for the U.K. is The Hyde Park FHC, 64-68 Exhibition Road, South Kensington, London, SW7 2PA (see map on page 34)**. The larger Centres, which I have indicated with an asterisk, do have copies of part of the indexes in stock and they can request others from the USA. The International Genealogical Index (IGI) compiled by the LDS is also available in many libraries within the UK.

Before calling at any of the Centres, please telephone first to find out the opening times. The LDS Family Service Centre in Birmingham kindly supplied the following information. (1881 British Census and National Index. England, Scotland, Wales, Channel Islands, Isle of Man and Royal Navy are available from the Church of the Latter Day Saints, 399 Garretts Green, Birmingham, B33 OUH. Price £29.75 (postage paid).

Aberdeen FHC, North Anderson Drive, Aberdeen, AB2 6DD, Grampian, Scotland.
Tel: 01224 692206

Aldershot FHC, LDS Chapel, St. Georges Road, Aldershot, Hants.
Tel: 01252 321460

Ashton FHC, Tweedale Street, Rochdale, Lancs. OL11 3TZ.
Tel: 01706 526292

Belfast FHC, 403 Holywood Road, Belfast, BT4 2GU.
Northern Ireland.
Tel: 028 9076 8250

*Billingham FHC, The Linkway, Billingham, Cleveland, TS23 3HJ.
Tel: 01642 563162

Blackpool FHC, LDS Chapel, Warren Drive, Blackpool, Lancs.
Tel: 01253 858218

*Bristol FHC, Brook Road, Bristol, Wilts. BS14 9HU.
Tel: 01225 777097

Canterbury FHC, LDS Chapel, Forty-Acre Road, Canterbury, Kent.
Tel: 01227 765431

Cambridge FHC, 670 Cherry Hinton Road, Cambridge, CB1 4DR.
Tel: 01223 247000

Cardiff FHC, Heol y Deri, Rhiwbina, Cardiff, South Glamorgan, CF4 6UH.
Tel: 029 2062 5342

Carlisle FHC, Langrigg Road, Morton Park, Carlisle, Cumbria. CA2 5HT.
Tel: 01228 26767 **(temp. closed)**

*Cheltenham FHC, Thirlestaine Road, Cheltenham, Glos.GI53 7AA.
Tel: 01242 523433

Chester FHC, 50 Cliftone Drive, Blacone, Chester, Cheshire, CH1 5LT.
Tel: 01244 390796

Chorley FHC, 33-41 Water Street, Chorley, Lancs.
Tel: 01257 233687

Coventry FHC, Riverside Close, Whitley, Coventry.
Tel: 024 7630 1420

*Crawley FHC, Old Horsham Road, Crawley, Sussex. RH11 8PD.
Tel: 01293 516151 **(temp. closed)**

Douglas FHC, Woodside-Woodburn Road, Isle of Man.
Tel: 01624 675834

Dublin FHC, Ireland Dublin Mission, The Willows, Finglas, Dublin, 11, Ireland.
Tel: 00 3531 830 9960

Dumfries FHC, 36 Edinburgh Road, Albanybank, Dumfries, Scotland.
Tel: unknown **(temp. closed)**

Dundee FHC, Bingham Terrace, Dundee, Tayside, DD4 7HH, Scotland.
Tel: 01382 451247

Edinburgh FHC, 30A, Colinton Road, Edinburgh, Scotland.
Tel: 0131 337 3049

Elgin FHC, Pansport Road, Elgin, Morayshire, IV3D. Scotland.
Tel: 01343 546429

Exeter FHC, Wonford Road, off Barrack Road, Exeter, Devon. EX2.
Tel: 013922 50723

Forest of Dean FHC, Wynols Hill, Queensway, Colesford, Gloucestershire.
Tel: 01594 832904

Gaerwen FHC, Holyhead Road, Gaerwen, Anglesey.
Tel: 01248 421894

Glasgow FHC, 35 Julian Avenue, Glasgow, Strathclyde, G12 ORB.
Tel: 0141 357 1024

Grimsby FHC, Grimsby Ward Chapel, Linwood Avenue, Waltham Road, Grimsby, Humberside. DN33 2PA.
Tel: 01472 828876

Harborne FHC, 38 Lordswood Road, Harborne, Birmingham, B17 9QB.
Tel: 0121 553 2137

Hastings FHC, 2 Ledsham Avenue, St. Leonards-on-Sea, East Sussex.
Tel: 01424 754563

Helston FHC, Clodgey Lane, Helston, Cornwall.
Tel: 01326 564503

Hereford FHC, 262 Kings Acre Road, Hereford.
Tel: 01432 352751

*Huddersfield FHC, 12 Halifax Street, Dewsbury, Yorks.
Tel: 01484 454573

Hull FHC, 725 Holderness Road, Hull, Yorks. HU4 7RT.
Tel: 01482 572623 **(temp. closed)**

Inverness FHC, 13 Ness Walk, Inverness, Scotland, IV3 5SQ.
Tel: 01463 231220

Ipswich FHC, 42 Sidegate Lane West, Ipswich, Suffolk. 1PA 3DB.
Tel: 01473 723182

Kilmarnock FHC, Whatriggs Road, Kilmarnock, Ayrshire, KA1 3QY.
Tel: 015635 26560

Kings Lynn FHC, Reffley Lane, Kings Lynn, Norfolk. PE30 3EQ.
Tel: 01553 670000

Kirkcaldy FHC, Winifred Crescent/Forth Park, Kirkcaldy, Fife, Scotland.
Tel: 01592 640041

Lancaster FHC, Lancaster Ward House, Overangle Road, Morecombe, Lancaster. LA1.
Tel: 01524 33571

Leeds FHC, Vesper Road, Leeds, West Yorkshire. LS5 3QT.
Tel: 01532 585297 **(temp. closed)**

Leicester FHC, Wakerley Road,
Leicester, LE5 4WD.
Tel: 01162 737334

Lerwick FHC, South Road,
Lerwick, Zer Orq. Shetland.
Tel: 01595 695732

Lowestoft FHC, 165 Yarmouth Road,
Lowestoft, Suffolk. NR32.
Tel: 01502 573851

Luton FHC, London Road,
at Cutenhoe Road, Luton, Bed.
Tel: 01582 482234

Maidstone FHC, 76B London Road,
Maidstone, Kent. ME16 ODR.
Tel: 01622 757811

Manchester FHC, Altrincham Road,
Wythenshawe, Manchester, M22 4BJ.
Tel: 0161 9029279

Mansfield FHC, Southridge Drive,
Mansfield, Nottinghamshire. NG18 4RT.
Tel: 01623 26729

Merthyr Tydfil FHC, Nanty Gwenith
Street, George Town, Merthyr Tydfil,
Wales.
Tel: 01685 722455

*Newcastle FHC, Cardigan Road,
Newcastle, Dyfed.
Tel: 01239 711473

*Newcastle-under-Lyme FHC,
 PO Box 457, The Brampton, Newcastle-
under-Lyme, Staffs. ST5 OTV.
Tel: 0178 262 0653

Newport FHC, Chestnut Close,
Shide Road, Newport, Isle of Wight.
Tel: 01983 529643

Northampton FHC,
137 Harlestone Road,
Northampton, NN5.
Tel: 0160 458 7630

Norwich FHC, 19 Greenways, Eaton,
Norwich. NR4 7AX.
Tel: 01603 452440

Nottingham FHC, Stanhome Square,
West Bridgeford, Nottingham. NG6 8PA.
Tel: 0115 9144255

Orpington FHC, Station Approach,
Orpington, Kent. BR6 OSX.
Tel: 01689 837342

Paisley FHC, Glenburn Road, Paisley.
Renfrewshire. PA2. Scotland.
Tel: 0141 884 2780

Peterborough FHC, Cottesmore Close,
Off Atherstone Avenue, Natherton Estate,
Peterborough.
Tel: 01733 263374

Plymouth FHC, Hartley Chapel,
Mannamead Road, Plymouth, Devon.
PL3.
Tel: 01752 668666

Pontefract FHC, Park Villas Drive,
Pontefract.
Tel: 01977 600308

Poole FHC, 8 Mount Road, Parkstone,
Poole, Dorset. BH14 OQW.
Tel: 01202 730646

Portsmouth FHC, Kingston Crescent,
Portsmouth, Hants.
Tel: 023 9269 6243

Rawtenstall FHC, Haslingden Road,
Rawtenstall, Rossendale, Lancs.
Tel: 01706 213460

Reading FHC, 280 The Meadway,
Tilehurst,
Reading, Berks.
Tel: 01189 410211

Redditch FHC, 321 Eversham Road,
Crabbs Cross, Redditch, Worcs. B97 5JA.
Tel: 01527 550657

Rhyl FHC, Rhuddlan Road, Rhyl,
Clwyd, Wales.
Tel: 01745 331172

Romford FHC, 64 Butts Green Road,
Hornchurch, Essex. RM11 2JJ.
Tel: unknown (**temp. closed**)

Scarborough FHC, Stepheny Drive/
Whitby Road, Scarborough,
North Humberside.
Tel: 01723 501026

Sheffield FHC, Wheel Lane, Glenoside,
Sheffield, Yorkshire. S30 3RL.
Tel: 0114 245 3124

St. Austell FHC, Kingfisher Drive,
St. Austell, Cornwall.
Tel: 01726 69912

St. Helier FHC, Rue de la Vallee,
St. Mary, St. Helier, Jersey,
Channel Islands.
I: 01534 482171

Staines FHC, 41 Kingston Road,
Staines, Middlesex. TW14 ONO.
Tel: 01784 462627

Stevenage FHC, Buckthorne Avenue,
Stevenage, Hertfordshire. SG1 1T.
Tel: 01438 351553

Sunderland FHC, Linden Road,
Off Queen Alexander Road,
Sunderland, Tyne & Wear.
Tel: 0191 5285787

Sutton Coldfield FHC, 185 Penns Lane,
Sutton Coldfield, Birmingham. B76 1JU.
Tel: 0121 386 1690

Swansea FHC, Crockett Road,
Swansea, West Glamorgan, Wales.
Tel: 01792 585792

Telford FHC, 72 Glebe Street,
Wellington, Salop.
Tel: 01952 257443

Thetford FHC, LDS Chapel,
Station Road, Thetford, Norfolk.
Tel: 01842 755472

Wandsworth FHC, 149 Nightingale Lane,
Balham, London, S.W.12.
Tel: 020 8673 6741

Watford FHC, Hempstead Road,
Watford, Herts.
Tel: 01923 251471

Wednesfield FHC, Linthouse Lane,
Wednesfield, Wolverhampton, West
Midlands.
Tel: 01902 724 097

Worthing FHC, Goring Street, Worthing,
West Sussex.
Tel: 01903 765790

Yate FHC, Wellington Road, Yate, Avon.
Tel: 01454 323004

Yeovil FHC, LDS Chapel, Forest Hill,
Yeovil, Somerset.
Tel: 01935 26817

York FHC, West Bank, Acomb, York,
Yorkshire.
Tel: 01904 785128

The Jewish Genealogical Society of Great Britain

- Valuable expert guidance in research.

- Regular gatherings to meet others interested in genealogy.

- Access to our growing library.

- SHEMOT and NEWSLETTER, our quarterly publications, full of helpful advice and information.

- Information on other societies all over the world and access to thousands of people interested in Jewish Genealogy.

- Use of the International Jewish Family Finder available at meetings.

- Information on our web-site and our e-mail messaging system.

- Access to our own Family Finder giving names being researched by our members.

Join us for an exciting journey discovering your personal family history. Begin by interviewing relatives, studying old photographs and family documents and then.... What next?

Our Society was formed in 1992 with beginners and experienced researchers joining forces.

- to help one another to learn and discover more about genealogy.

- to encourage genealogical research.

- to promote the preservation of Jewish genealogical records and resources.

- to share information amongst members.

The Society is open to all interested in Jewish genealogy and is constituted on a wholly secular basis.

We have a regular programme of events, including lectures with specialist speakers, visits to genealogical sources, and meetings in members' homes. Special Interest Groups research particular localities and the art of writing a Family History. Our annual all-day seminar attracts excellent speakers, well known as experts in their fields. Regional meetings are also arranged.

We lead the Family History Workshops held by the Jewish Museum at the Sternberg Centre in Finchley, and at other venues.

We also provide speakers for educational meetings at schools and synagogues and panels for social events, often in conjunction with other charities.

Our journal, SHEMOT (names), was the 1998 winner of the International Association of Jewish Genealogical Societies' Outstanding Publication award. Published quarterly, it contains a variety of articles of interest to genealogists, book reviews, abstracts of overseas genealogical journals, practical research tips, and useful addresses. We are keen to publish members' own articles.

We have a lively *Newsletter*, also published quarterly, giving news about the Society and forthcoming events, international genealogical affairs, computer activities, including our web site, library notes, members' letters and queries and lists of new members.

Our reference library of books, research papers, microfiches and journals from other societies around the world is being built up. It includes one of the largest collection of *Yizkor* (memorial) books in the U.K., covering many of the destroyed communities in Europe, and many family trees, indexed by principal surnames, compiled by our members. The library is open to members at regular times announced in advance.

Our web site, www.ort.org/jgsgb, has pages covering the programme, membership, *Shemot*, (including a list of published articles), the library (including the catalogue), useful links, and a repository of files contributed by members and available for down-loading.

We have two e-mail addresses: jgsgb@ort.org for general enquiries and jgsgbmem.@org.ort for membership related enquiries. An electronic mailing list has also been set up, so that messages can easily (and extremely cheaply) be sent to every member on the list, whilst preserving their anonymity.

The Society is run by volunteers who give time, effort and expertise. We can always use more help.

We cannot undertake paid research, but we can give general advice and sometimes help with specific points of difficulty. Genealogical enquiries may be sent to:

The Genealogical Enquiries Officer
The Jewish Genealogical Society of Great Britain
PO Box 13288
LONDON N3 3WD

The Jewish Genealogical Society of Great Britain

APPLICATION FOR MEMBERSHIP

Surname ....

Forename ....

Address ....

....

.... Postcode..

Telephone ....Fax ....

E-mail address ....

To join please send a remittance made payable to The Jewish Genealogical Society of Great Britain to the Membership Secretary

Membership (*see over*) £ ....

Donation £ ....

...... copies of the Beginner's Guide
(£4.50 U.K., £6.00 or US$ 10.00 overseas) £ ....

Back numbers of *Shemot (see below)*

Pack A   1993 - 1994   No of packs _____   £ ....

Pack B   1995 - 1996   No of packs _____   £ ....

Pack C   1997 - 1998   No of packs _____   £ ....

Single copies *(please state which)* £ ....

TOTAL £_____

Back numbers of *SHEMOT* are available as packs of eight issues, which cost £24.00 for each pack for despatch to U.K. addresses, £27.00 (UK cheques or sterling drafts) or US$44.00 (other cheques or drafts) for overseas, or as single copies, which cost £4.00 each for U.K. addresses, £5.00 or US$8.00 for overseas.

The Society is a Registered Charity No 1022738
To covenant your subscription, please contact the Membership Secretary   *(see over)*

Subscriptions

	January to December	July to December	October to December next year
Individual	£20.00	£10.00	£25.00
Family (two people, one copy of *SHEMOT*, etc)	£25.00	£12.50	£31.25
Reduced rate - full time student or registered unemployed	£10.00	£ 5.00	£12.50
Overseas - UK cheques and sterling drafts	£25.00	£12.50	£31.25
Overseas - other cheques and drafts	US$ 54.00	US$ 33.00	US$ 65.00

Confidentiality

We circulate a membership list to members only, to help those with similar interests to contact each other more easily. Those who do not wish the list to include their names, addresses, telephone and fax numbers and e-mail addresses should indicate below. Where details are withheld, a forwarding service, using the Society's Post Office box number, is available.

I wish my telephone and fax numbers and e-mail address to be withheld ☐

I wish my address, telephone and fax numbers and e-mail address to be withheld ☐

I wish my name and other details to be omitted from the list altogether ☐

Speeding the Mail

I would like to have my copies of the *NEWSLETTER*, membership lists, the family finder and members' bookshelves sent to me by E-mail ☐

How did you hear of the Society?

....

Signature ....

Please return this form, together with your remittance, to:

The Membership Secretary,
The Jewish Genealogical Society of Great Britain,
2 Milton Close, London, N2 OQH.

November 1999

READING HEADSTONES
Derek Wenzerul

Many people find it difficult to interpret the symbols and Hebrew inscriptions on headstones. Below are various [1]icons and symbols used on headstones. In addition there are details of the [2]Hebrew alphabet with numerical values, the months of the Hebrew year, day of the month numbers in Hebrew and English. and some [3]Hebrew abbreviations.

The Jewish year numbering system runs from an earlier date than the Christianity based secular date. The Jewish year 5760 commenced at around sunset on Sep 10 1999 C.E.

Interpreting Symbols on Graves
Reprinted with permission from the Historical Oakland Cemetery Inc

Jewish iconography, as well as symbols which Jews borrowed from other traditions has been adapted for this use. Below is a key to some of the most common icons with descriptions to help interpret them.

The raised hands indicate that the deceased was a Kohen, a descendant of Aaron and the High Priests who officiated in the ancient Temple.

Masonic symbols are quite common among Jewish graves since they were active in such local fraternal orders. Military insignias are found on markers of veterans who died in service.

The pitcher and basin mark the grave of a Levi, a descendant of the Biblical tribe which assisted the High Priests as Temple functionaries.

A branch with a plucked leaf or a tree with broken limbs represents a life cut short.

The *Magen David* or Star of David is the most universal sign of the Jewish people today. It was popularised with the advent of the Zionist movement in the late 19th century.

The veil, a symbol used widely on Victorian markers, was made to resemble a *tallit* or prayer shawl. An urn with such a veil draped over it resembles a Jewish man bent in worship.

Shemot, Volume 4, 2 — 13

References
1   *Shemot*, Vol.4/2, p.13, 1996
2   JGSGB Seminar - handout
3   IAJGS Cemetery Project web site

Gravestone Symbols

Candelabra: Signifies a woman.

Six pointed star: (Magen David, The Shield of David) which usually signifies an Israelite man, but also can appear on women's graves.

Two Hand with Four Fingers: Divided in two sets of two fingers each, signifies a Cohen, a Temple Priest.

Pitcher: Signifies a Levite, who was responsible for cleaning the hands of the Temple Priest before they performed their priestly duties.

HEBREW ALPHABET AND NUMERIC VALUES			FINAL FORM
1	Aleph	א	
2	Bet	ב	
3	Gimel	ג	
4	Dalet	ד	
5	Hay	ה	
6	Vav	ו	
7	Zayin	ז	
8	Khet	ח	
9	Tet	ט	
10	Yud	י	
20	Chuf	כ	ך
30	Lamed	ל	
40	Mem	מ	ם
50	Nun	נ	ן
60	Samech	ס	
70	Ayin	ע	
80	Pay	פ	ף
90	Tzade	צ	ץ
100	Kuf	ק	
200	Resh	ר	
300	Shin	ש	
400	Tav	ת	

Notes

Thousands, if written, is designated by a single quote next to the letter.

'א = 1000,   'ה = 5000.

A double quote between the last two letters signifies a year. תש"ו represents 706, and the year (5)706. (Thousands omitted).

Additional Reading: Susser.B, see Bibliography

English Months	Hebrew Months		Days of the month			
Sept/Oct	חשרי	Tishri	1	א	16	טז
Oct/Nov	חשון	Cheshvan	2	ב	17	יז
Nov/Dec	כסלו	Kislev	3	ג	18	יח
Dec/Jan	טבת	Tevet	4	ד	19	יט
Jan/Feb	שבט	Shevat	5	ה	20	כ
Feb/Mar	אדר	Adar	6	ו	21	כא
Mar	אדר בי	Adar II	7	ז	22	כב
Mar/Apr	ניסן	Nisan	8	ח	23	כג
Apr/May	אייר	Iyar	9	ת	24	כד
May/Jun	סיון	Sivan	10	י	25	כה
Jun/Jul	תמוז	Tammuz	11	יא	26	כו
Jul/Aug	אב	Av	12	יב	27	כז
Aug/Sep	אלול	Elul	13	יג	28	כח
			14	יד	29	כט
			15	טו	30	ל

Hebrew Abbreviations

פ"נ	(Poh Niqbar) Here lies buried
פ"ט	(Poh Nitman/Poh Tamon) Here lies interred
	(In UK usually פ"נ = male and פ"ט = female)
ר'	(Reb) Honorific (Does NOT mean Rabbi)
מרת	Mrs/Miss
בת	Daughter of
בן	Son of
ב'ר	(Ben/Bat Reb) Son/Daughter of
מו"ה	(Moreinu HaRav) Our Teacher, Rabbi
הכהן	The person was a Cohen
הלוי	The person was a Levi
ת'נ'צ'ב'ח	Acronym - May his/her soul be bound up in the bonds of (everlasting) life.
אברהם אבנו	Abraham our Father, Signifies a male convert
אמינו	Our Mother
ר"ח	Rosh Chodesh (New Month)
א'ר'ח	First day of the new month

YIZKOR BOOKS
Cyril Fox

The legacy of the Holocaust is enshrined in a series of Memorial (Yizkor) books. There are perhaps a thousand of these volumes, which testify to the barbarity and inhumanity of the Nazi Regime.

These books are usually in Yiddish or Hebrew, with occasional English articles. They contain photographs of the shtetl and its people, lists of those murdered and articles by survivors and relatives. The book is usually compiled by a committee of landsleit.

For the genealogist they are a prime source of information about our relatives in the "Heim". Much of this information remains to be unlocked but translations are proceeding, see especially JewishGen website www.jewishgen.org.(Yizkor book project Translations).

A list of Yizkor books in Great Britain will be found in the JGSGB Library, and it is hoped that this will be published. The British Library has around 250 such books and is also hoping to publish its list shortly.

The following libraries have collections: The Jewish Genealogical Society of Great Britain (JGSGB), Leopold Muller Memorial Library (Yarnton Manor), Jew's College (London School of Jewish Studies), Wiener Library, University College London (Jewish Section), School of Oriental & African Studies (SOAS), University of London (Stencl Collection), Parkes Library Southampton, British Library and Cambridge University Library.

A list of Yizkor books, shtetl by shtetl alphabetically, has been compiled by Zachary Baker and can be found in Arthur Kurzweil's book, *From Generation to Generation* (ISBN 0-06-273335-4 pbk).

MAKING THE MOST OF YOUR FAMILY HISTORY
Rosemary Wenzerul

Genealogy is a pastime, which may be left for years then resumed at any time in the future. Producing trees with many names and dates, although an achievement, can be rather boring. It is therefore so important to bring your tree to life. You can do this by breaking away from your standard tree and looking at other aspects of your family history.

If you break your family history down into appropriate sections, you can focus on your research and perhaps involve other people to help you. The headings suggested were most useful for my research but you may wish to include others. The sections should be arranged into some order, either chronological or alphabetical. Be as accurate as possible with dates and events and most of all add a bit of humour to your stories in order to make them more interesting.

FAMILY
If the family you are researching is very large with numerous children, break it down into sections showing each child and their families separately. If possible, include photographs in each section and as many stories as you can for each one. Should you wish to expand, include separate files on 'associated families' (in alphabetical order by surname).

BIRTHS
Include photographs of the family as babies (dated on reverse); The Jewish Chronicle or other regional newspaper insertion; Baby words; Their first lock of hair; Birthday parties held over the years - where they were held and who came to them; Any birth certificates you acquire (file in alphabetical order by surname); Grandparents could write about the pleasure of seeing their first grandchild and his/her progression to adulthood.

BARMITZVAH/BATMITZVAH
Use photographs of the event, the invitation, the table plan, memorabilia, etc. Write about the events of the day. You might want to include details of the synagogue, what portion was read and of course the Jewish Chronicle or other regional newspaper insertion/photograph if appropriate.

MARRIAGES
The name of the Synagogue where the wedding took place; The names of the persons who officiated; Photographs of wedding (if a group, name them from left to right); invitations; menus; marriage certificates (in alphabetical order by surname of bridegroom); ketubot (contract); table plan; memorabilia, etc.

Jewish weddings result in two pieces of paper, a marriage certificate and the ketubah (contract). If you have copies of both it is a good idea to file them together. Write about the events on the day and the build-up to the day; Jewish Chronicle or other regional newspaper insertion; Record memories of special anniversaries (silver weddings etc) and how you celebrated them, with whom and where, photographs (name and date).

GRAVES
If you visit cemeteries, take photographs of the graves. If you do not know the grave location, ask the cemetery office and record it. Also include under this heading the death certificates of all your family (filed in alphabetical order by surname); the inscription on the grave; Jewish Chronicle or other regional newspaper insertion and date of stone setting etc. If you have a date of death but no grave location you could always include copies of the burial record (this applies to old records).

SCHOOL/COLLEGE/UNIVERSITY
Describe the School/College location. It may still exist by name but may have moved several times. Include school reports, certificates, group photos of your class (name them including teachers), games you played e.g. hop scotch, skipping and the rhymes you put to them. Photocopy board games e.g. snakes and ladders, ludo etc and the instructions on how to play them. Write a list of the sweets you ate; the friends you made; the organisations you belonged to (e.g. scouts, guides) etc. The degree you obtained and the degree ceremony plus dated photograph of the occasion and your memories of the day.

EMPLOYMENT
What was the occupation of the family? Did they own a business? Did they have employees or did they work for someone else? You could include the names, dates and addresses of the places of work. Include any relevant documents: a curriculum vitae, contract of employment or letter of acceptance, job description, first pay slip, an account of the work, achievements and promotion, working environment and friends. After work there may be retirement parties, again with photos, including names and dates.

FAMILY AT WAR
Photographs of your family in uniform; where and when they served; the name of their regiment and service number if known; medals they won; call-up papers; letters they wrote to loved ones; stories of what happened to them during the War and of course what happened to the civilian member of the family. Memorabilia in general. If they were killed abroad, were they buried in one of the Commonwealth War Cemeteries - if so give details of Cemetery, location (photograph a map of the area), grave reference. Further details may be obtained from the Commonwealth War Grave Commission's web-site **(see page 33 for details)**.

FAMILY SAYINGS
Most families have their own sayings, some quite expressive! List them and explain what they mean, examples of when they were used and whose expressions they were.

FAMILY RECIPES
Almost all families have recipes, which have been handed down from generation to generation. It is so important for these to continue through future generations - so make the effort and write them out. If the finished recipe looks very appetising and is decorated, photograph it. Remember to record the origin and the name of the person who gave it.

PROPERTY
If you know where the family lived you may have pictures of the property. Photocopy a map of the area and highlight the road. If you have reduced the map be sure to say so and state the source so that the map can be found in the future. If the property still exists you could either photograph it yourself, or if it happens to be on the market, contact the estate agent for details. Include underground and bus maps covering the area (if not dated, date them). Make lists from birth, marriage and death certificates and from other sources the addresses of your family and the dates they lived there. Build up a picture of their lives. (Suggest you use a suitable computer program which will sort the information into different forms e.g. by surname first or address or by date).

FREEMASONRY
Were some of your family freemasons? If so include photographs and details of their Lodge etc. If you need more information, you can write to the United Grand Lodge of England, Freemasons' Hall, Great Queen Street, London, WC2B 5AZ for information. Unfortunately, they take between 4-6 months to reply!

HOBBIES
If your ancestor had an unusual hobby or was actively involved in sport, there could be certificates, newspaper write-ups or photographs of the occasions.

NEWSPAPERS
Keep cuttings of births, marriages and deaths relating to your family and ensure you record the date they appeared in the Jewish Chronicle, regional and local Jewish newspapers. If you have a family bible, enter the details into this too.

CORRESPONDENCE
Keep all correspondence relating to the research you have done in alphabetical/date order (by surname) for future reference.

REFERENCES
Make a separate file of any references you may acquire. For example, if you visit the Public Record Office or Newspaper Library, ask at reception for the leaflets giving details of the organisation and the opening times etc and keep on file for future reference.

PHOTOGRAPHS
Old photographs should be copied as the originals can fade and get damaged. It is very easy to scan and store them on a computer. If the photographs are in the

family album and the negatives are not available copying or re-photographing them can be done in situ without spoiling the album.

If you decide to photograph them, it is cheaper to use colour film and process it locally rather than purchasing black and white film unless you print it yourself. Against as many photographs as possible include a story however short it may be. Ensure you include the name, date, event and location against each photograph. If you wish to write on the reverse of your print, one can purchase a special pen from most camera shops that will not spoil the photograph. Always index and store your negatives carefully. Always create backup files on floppy discs.

MEMORABILIA
Start to collect memorabilia. It could be in the form of sweet wrappers; badges; plastic cards; brochures showing the produce/fashion prices in a specific year etc. Write articles about yourself - what hobbies do you have; the holidays you had as a child, did you return to the place that you loved as a child and were then disappointed that it was no longer the same. Did you see the total eclipse in 1999, if so, what were your feelings at the time. What were you and your family doing in the year 2000 - did the millennium bug attack you! If so, what happened? Report on the progress in industry and inventions you have seen during your lifetime and how it has improved your way of life. What are your views on, for example, genetically modified crops? Could they damage the environment in the future? Shops which no longer exist and what they sold. What are your feelings about the last 100 years - for example, the violence of the wars in this period?

DOCUMENT CARE
Always store your data in suitable sleeves, files etc. If you decide to use plastic folders ensure they are the ones that will not lift off the print.

However you decide to bring your family history to life, it is important to be as accurate as possible with the information you hold and, most important of all, to share the information you have with other researchers. The more names and information you can swap with others the more interesting and exciting genealogy becomes, as the more information you receive, the more links you are likely to make and tend to make new friends and relations along the way. Do remember to give credit to the researchers who provided you with the information. There is no race to finish your tree, as this is a never-ending pastime. You may not be able to go any further backwards in time, but future generations are continuing and it is for future generations that your family history is aimed, so ensure that you enjoy what you are doing and make your family history as interesting, humorous and informative a pastime as possible. I reiterate: with genealogy, it is so important to remember to help one another as much as possible and reciprocate with as much information as possible when data is sent to you.

DRAWING YOUR FAMILY TREE
Rosemary Wenzerul

Once you have sufficient information, it is time to prepare your family tree. This requires extreme accuracy and patience as it is usually after several attempts you will eventually succeed!

As you will see from the following examples, there are many ways in which trees may take form. The style of your tree will be entirely up to you. The three examples shown on the following pages are all correct. If you feel you are unable to draw one then you can purchase some very attractive printed ones. Adverts for these are in most genealogical magazines or may be obtained from the [1]Society of Genealogists (who also sell genealogical magazines). Alternatively, most genealogical software packages (e.g. Brothers Keeper or Family Tree Maker) will do this too (see section on computers).

So returning to drawing up your tree. You will need an A3 (12"x17"/30cmx43cm) piece of paper, or graph paper if you prefer. As you are likely to make mistakes, it would be advisable to use a pencil/ruler and have an eraser handy. An A3 piece of paper should be able to incorporate four generations (the fourth generation being the great-grandchild of the person(s) shown at the top centre of your tree). So start with yourself and work backwards as per examples. Only work with one family at a time. If you make a mistake, you can always erase it and once the tree is correct and you are happy with the presentation, you can then go over it in ink.

Ideally you need to include the full name, date of birth(b), marriage(m) and death(d) against each person's name. This obviously depends on the amount of information available. If you haven't got all this information, do still start your tree by filling in all the names; you can always add information to it at a later date. All dates should be recorded in full (e.g. 21 March 1881) or if you are unsure of the exact year it may be shown as c.1881 (c=circa).

Children are usually shown left to right with the eldest child being shown on the left.

Once you have finished your paternal line, it is usual to start on your maternal line.

The above is a start and you will find that once you have completed the tree as far as you can, you will probably wish to enlarge on it. There is no rush to do this as genealogy is an on-going pastime and you can pick up where you left off at any time in the future.

It is important to be as accurate and methodical as possible with the information you record and to try to keep your tree up-to-date for future generations.

[1] Society of Genealogists - see section on useful addresses.

Box Chart

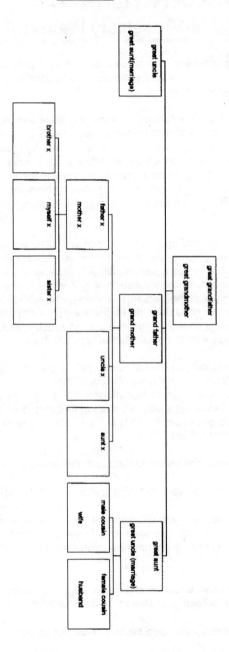

Tree Chart

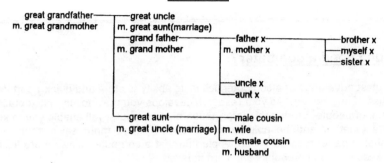

```
great grandfather──────┐ great uncle
m. great grandmother   │ m. great aunt(marriage)
                       ├──grand father──────────┐ father x───────────────┐ brother x
                       │  m. grand mother        │ m. mother x            ├─myself x
                       │                         │                        └─sister x
                       │                         ├──uncle x
                       │                         └──aunt x
                       └──great aunt─────────────┐ male cousin
                          m. great uncle (marriage) m. wife
                                                  ├──female cousin
                                                  m. husband
```

Wheel Chart

51

USING A COMPUTER IN GENEALOGY
Joe Ross

Why do I need a computer?

The biggest advantage of a computer lies in its ability to store and quickly sort large quantities of information. As your research develops you may accumulate details of hundreds of people. Storing this information on a computer will enable you to keep the data together and be able to share it with others more easily than using conventional paper records. Most people find that a computer allows more flexible record keeping than notebooks and card indexes.

Family trees take a long time to draw by hand and can be hard to update. However a good computer genealogy program can draw a variety of styles of trees within a few seconds. Modern programs also allow you to incorporate photographs in your tree.

The Internet provides access to a wealth of information. Much of this information is not readily available in Great Britain and, before the advent of the Internet, would have been impractical to access. In addition the Internet offers the opportunity to correspond electronically by email with others throughout the world at a fraction of the cost and with an immediacy not available by conventional mail.

What can I use a computer for?

Interview notes and record keeping
Use a word processor to type up interview notes and compile simple indexes of documents. Most computers come with some sort of word processor (a writing package). Often, these packages allow you to combine tables, pictures and text in your writing.

Information about people
Keep all of your information about people and their relationships in a Family History Program. Such programs are written specifically for genealogists and are designed to handle large amounts of data. These can produce a variety of family trees, reports and even mini family books. Photographs and documents can also be stored. However, these first have to be transferred into the computer using an add-on device called a scanner which is useful for those with more computing experience.

A special style of genealogical file (Gedcom) has been developed which allows people to transfer their data between different genealogical computer programs, thus enabling them to share information.

The Internet
The Internet is, in effect, a way of linking computers all around the world using satellite and cable links. The term World Wide Web (WWW) is another name often used for the Internet. Before you can link your home computer to this network the computer will need to

☐ be registered with an Internet Service Provider (ISP) for example freeserve or demon. These companies allow access to the Internet via their computer and satellite relays. They also have space to store any web pages you may produce to create your own home page. An email address will be allocated when registering with your ISP (e.g. harry@cs.com).

☐ have Internet software installed - such as Netscape or Microsoft Internet Explorer. These programs sometimes referred to as browsers, allow you to view the information on the Internet.

Reference databases
Many databases of genealogical information are available on the Internet, or can be purchased as CD-ROMs. For example the U.S. Social Security Death Index, the U.K. census for 1881, the Cemetery Project Database (from the International Association of Jewish Genealogical Societies - IAJGS).

Why Use the Internet?

Electronic mail
It is easy to exchange messages by email with family members and others who can assist with your research. Messages can be sent worldwide almost instantaneously - generally for the cost of a local call. This is done using an emailing program into which you type your message and your recipients email address.

Browsing the World Wide Web -'surfing the net'
Many organisations, including The Jewish Genealogical Society of Great Britain (JGSGB), maintain web pages that are full of information for the genealogist. For example, the JGSGB website contains lists of names of insertions of deaths in the Jewish Chronicle, a few cemetery indexes e.g. the Bristol cemetery and catalogues of its magazine *Shemot* and library holdings.

For Jewish information, one of the best sources is an International voluntary site called JewishGen. This has a very comprehensive website dedicated to Jewish Genealogy. An important service they provide allows you to get in touch with other people, who may be situated anywhere in the world, researching the same surname or town.

Often private individuals, who in the past would not have been able to produce books or articles, publish their research on their own web pages, or links they have found which have helped them. For example Cindy's List is a website which contains thousands of links to websites of interest to the genealogist.

Newsgroups

Newsgroups are set up for people with special interests and hobbies to share ideas. They are rather like electronic notice boards on which people can leave messages. The principal newsgroup relevant to Jewish genealogists is operated by JewishGen and is called soc.genealogy.jewish.

An individual can post (send by email) a query or comment for inclusion on the newsgroup. Each item has a title. When running your newsgroup software (part of your internet software) you will see a list of all the recent titles of postings. It is then your choice to select the areas of interest.

You can post a follow up article/posting of your own or write directly by email to the person who posted the original.

There are thousands of newsgroups on the Internet. Many, like JewishGen, are moderated. This means that all postings are rigorously vetted. Be warned that there are unmoderated newsgroups that may carry biased views or may promote obscene correspondence.

Mailing lists

These provide a facility whereby email messages can be sent to hundreds of people who are pursuing a common interest. The JGSGB operates its own mailing list; full details on how to join are provided to members.

Mailing lists are a useful way to keep people in touch with events. The messages sent to the JGSGB mailing list serve as a form of continuous discussion between members.

What type of computer do I require?

Any current model of personal computer may be purchased, as genealogy does not normally require a machine that is particularly large or powerful unless one is planning to scan in large numbers of complex documents or photographs.

Portable or desk model, screen size

If short of space or require to take the computer to libraries/meetings, consider a portable rather than a desk model. Portables cost roughly 50% more. If deciding on a desk model, think carefully about the choice of screen size (15" or 17"). A 17" screen is very clear to use but requires a desk 90cm deep for comfort.

Backup device

A very common disaster is to lose all of one's data due to some kind of failure. It is therefore worth investing in a backup device. The most common type is known as a zip drive. This is a special type of disk drive, which has a removable high capacity cartridge. It is a good idea to store a copy of your files onto this drive every few days or so. Then remove the zip cartridge and put it somewhere safe, away from your computer.

Printer
Choice of printer is largely determined by how much you want to pay - clarity of print and speed are the determining factors.

Modem
If access to the Internet is required, you will need a modem to link your computer to the telephone system.

Software
This information on software is targeted at PC users. If wishing to use an older computer or prefer an Apple Mac computer, you will need to take advice about which software programs the computer can run.

A simple word processor, such as Microsoft Works, may be included in the price of some PCs. If you want to produce more complex documents then Microsoft Word or similar is recommended.

There are a number of family history programs available. Many JGSGB members consider Family Tree Maker (Broderbund Software) easy to use. The de luxe edition includes some CD-ROMs, which contain reference databases. The Society of Genealogists **(see pages 35, 57)** sells a range of family history programs at competitive prices.

Suppliers
Some suppliers sell the hardware cheaply but try to make their money by selling expensive software and other services. So make your price comparisons on the total for all of the hardware and software and cables and installation assistance that you require. A supplier should be found who will install the software for you - including that required for the Internet. Unpacking a computer from the box is not difficult, but it is a lot easier if you have done it before! So you may prefer to use a supplier who offers an installation service (albeit for a small fee). It is a matter of personal preference whether to purchase from a shop where computers are demonstrated, or try to obtain a cheaper machine from a mail order company.

How do I get started on the Internet?

Part of the Internet software on your computer is a browsing program (often Internet Explorer or Netscape).
Type in the address of the website which you want to see. Three useful websites that contain links to lots of other websites are:
www.ort.org/jgsgb for the JGSGB
www.jewishgen.org for Jewishgen
www.CyndisList.com for Cindy's list

Search engines
Search engines make it possible to locate articles on virtually any topic. Your computer will be set up to use some common search engines, or you can type in their address yourself (e.g. www.excite.co.uk).

You can look for articles on specific topics (e.g. try searching on Jewish Genealogy) or perhaps search for an unusual surname to see if there articles which mention it. Search engines can be used to track down web pages of record offices and the like (e.g. try searching on public record office). Such web pages often provide useful information as to holdings, admission regulations etc. Many sites also have their own search engines - look for something that says, "Search" or "search this site".

Databases of other researchers
There are many specialised genealogy databases that can help you to see if others are tracing similar families. The JewishGen website has the JGFF (Jewish Genealogical Family Finder) which lists surnames and places being searched. It also has the FTJP (Family Tree of the Jewish People), which contains complete family trees in electronic form.

The First Steps:

Before you buy your own computer try out some of these suggestions on somebody else's. Most large public libraries offer Internet and word processing facilities at a low "per hour" rate. Often there are staff available to assist (who may also offer formal courses). If you live in North London, a visit to the Hendon Multimedia Centre (see below) is highly recommended. The Society of Genealogists (see below) run courses and seminars on the subject of computers and genealogy.

Do not be afraid to seek assistance from a knowledgeable friend. It may be awkward to ask but it will save a lot of effort.

Useful Addresses:

The Hendon Multimedia Centre
Hendon Library,
The Burroughs,
London NW4.
Tel: 020 8359 2628 or 2629

The Society of Genealogists
14 Charterhouse Buildings,
Goswell Road, London EC1M 7BA **(See map on page 35)**
Tel: 020 7251 8799

GOING FURTHER AFIELD (EUROPE AND ELSEWHERE)
Saul Issroff

Although this Guide is aimed at research in the British Isles, the following addresses and information may be of help to beginners who are tracing their family abroad. Within The Jewish Genealogical Society of Great Britain (JGSGB) there are also sub-groups that specialise in researching individual countries and where everyone learns much from each other. Special Interest Groups (SIGs) for Latvia, Lithuania, Poland with Galicia, German speaking areas and for the United Kingdom itself have already been formed. These are expected to expand and develop further. Dates and times of the meetings are given in the JGSGB Newsletter. In addition, SIGs are mentioned on www.jewishgen where a lot of very useful information is located.

AUSTRALIA

Australian Archives
Queen Victoria Terrace, Canberra, Australia.
(Postal address) PO Box 7425, Canberra Mail Centre, ACT 2610, Australia.
Tel: 02 6209 3633 - Fax: 02 6209 3931

National Library of Australia
(Postal address) Canberra, ACT 2600, Australia.
Tel: 02 6260 1111
E-mail: http://www.nla.gov.au

AUSTRIA

Jewish Museum Wien
Seitenstettengasse 4, A-1010 Vienna. Austria.

BELARUS

Central State Historical Archive of Belarus
u. Kozlova 26, 220038 Minsk, Belarus.

CANADA

The National Archives of Canada
395 Wellington Street, Ottowa, KIA ON3, Canada.

DENMARK

Danish National Archives
Rigsdagsgarden 9,
DK 1218 Kobenhaven, K.
Denmark.
Tel: (45) 33923310 - Fax: (45) 33153239

GERMANY

(Births, Marriages and Death Register Offices)
Senatsverwaltung fur Inneres in Berlin
IC 506/507, Fehrbelliner Platz, D-10702 Berlin.
There is no central registry office for Berlin, but each district has its own.
If the exact address of the district is not known, the above address may be of use.
There is a charge for each enquiry, which may take several months.

Landesarchiv Berlin
Kalckreuthstrasse 1-2, D-10777 Berlin.

Lists of Berlin deportations including documentation of seizure of assets etc.
Various other material on Jewish and the Jewish community of Berlin.

Jewish Cemetery in Berlin Weissensee
Herbert-Baum-Strasse 45, D-13088 Berlin-Weissensee.

The administration of the Jewish cemetery has complete records of all graves on this cemetery, which opened in September 1880 as well as most for the old Jewish cemetery Berlin, Schonhauser Allee (1827-1880). Some burials in family plots took place after this. For some burials particulars of next of kin are also held.

State Archive Stuttgart
Konrad-Adenauerstrasse 4, D-70137 Stuttgart.

Generallandesarchiv Karlsruhe
Nordliche Hildapromenade 2, D076133 Karlsruhe.

HOLLAND

Register Amsterdam
Stadhouderskade 85, Amsterdam, Holland.
Tel: 0031 (0) 20 5519 911
Web-site: www.amsterdam.nl

ISRAEL

Central Archives for the History of the Jewish People
PO Box 1149, 91010 Jerusalem, Israel.
(Worldwide focus, but strong collections on French, Italian, German and Austrian Jewry. Only scattered records from Eastern Europe).
Tel: 00 972 2 635 716

Jewish National and University Library
PO Box 503, Jerusalem 91004, Israel.
Tel: 00 972 2 660351
Department of Manuscripts: Tel: 00 972 2 585 0555
Microfilm Room: Tel: 00 972 2 585 0222

Search Bureau for Missing Persons
HaSochnut HaYehudi, PO Box 92, Jerusalem, Israel.
Tel: +2-6202652 - Fax: +2-6202893

Yad Vashem Martyrs and Heroes Remembrance Authority
PO Box 3477, Jerusalem 91034, Israel,
(Archives, library and Hall of Names. The ultimate resource for Holocaust research)

LATVIA

Central State Historical Archives
Slokas Jela 16, LV-1007, Riga, Latvia.

LITHUANIA

Lietuvos Valstybinis Istorijos Archyvas
(Lithuanian State Historical Archives)
Gerosios Vilties 10, Vilnius 2015, Lithuania.
(Holds records for before 1895)

Centrinis Valstybinis Civilnis Metrikacijos Archyvas
Kalinausko St. 21, Vilnius, Lithuania.
(Holds vital records for 1895-1940)

POLAND

Naczelna Dyrekcja Archiwow Panstwowych
ul. Dluga 6, Skr. Pocztowa Nr 1005, 00-950 Warszawa, Poland.
(Records over 100 years old are located throughout a dozen-plus regional archives, but write to main archives listed above). Records less than 100 years old are still stored at the local Civil Registrar's office.
Write to: Urzad Stanu Cywilnego, (Your Town), Poland.
(They may or they may not be responsive).

ROMANIA

Archivelor Statului din Republica Romania
Bdul Kogalniceanu nr. 29, Buceresti, Sect 5, Romania.

SLOVAKIA

Statny Ustredny Archiv
Cesta 42, Bratislava, Slovakia.

SOUTH AFRICA

Central Archives Depot, Private Bag X236, Pretoria, 0001 RSA.

Cape Archives Depot, Private Bag X9025, Cape Town, 8000 RSA.

Department of Home Affairs
Private Bag X114, Pretoria, 0001 (vital records) RSA.

UKRAINE

Central State Historical Archives of Ukraine
u. Solomenskaya 24, 252601 Kiev, Ukraine.
Tel: (044) 227 3002

U.S.A

American Jewish Archives   (American Jewry)
3101 Clifton Avenue, Cincinnati, OH. 45220. U.S.A.

American Jewish Historical Society   (American Jewry)
2 Thornton Road,
Waltham, NA. 02154. U.S.A.
The AJHS is relocating the major portion of its collections to the Center for Jewish History, 15 West 16th Street, New York, NY 10011. Most of their catalogues are accessible on: http://www.ajhs.org/libarch.htm

Leo Baeck Institute   (German Jewry)
129 East 73rd Street, New York. NY. 10021. U.S.A.

Church of the Latter Day Saints (Mormons)
Family History Library,
30 East North Temple Street, Salt Lake City, UT. 84150, U.S.A.

Naturalisation Records
Immigration and Naturalisation Service,
FOIA/PA Section, Room 5114, 425 Eye Street, N.W.
Washington, DC. 20530. U.S.A.

Passenger Lists
General Reference Branch,
U.S. National Archives, 7th Pennsylvania Avenue,
N.W. Washington, DC. 20408. U.S.A.

Passports
(Before 1925 - National Archives. After 1925 see below)
U.S. State Department, Passport Office,
Bureau of Consular Affairs, FAIM/RS Room 1239,
22nd and C Streets, Washington, DC. 20520.

U.S. National Archives
8th and Pennsylvania Avenue, N.W. Washington, DC. 20408.

YIVO Institute   (Central and East
15 West 16th Street,   European Jewry)
New York, NY. 10011. U.S.A.
Tel: 212 246 6080 - Fax: 212 292 1892
E-mail: vivo1@metgate.metro.org

Irma and Paul Milstein Division of United States History
Local History and Genealogy,
The New York Public Library,
Humanities and Social Science Library, Room 315S,
Fifth Avenue and 42nd Street, New York, NY 10018, U.S.A.
Tel: 212 930 0828
Web-site: http://www.nypl.org/research/chss/lhg/genea.html

LISTS OF JEWISH GENEALOGICAL SOCIETIES WORLDWIDE

The International Association of Jewish Genealogical Societies (IAJGS) represents
over 80 societies worldwide and lists can be obtained:

Via Mail: Send a self-addressed stamped envelope to:
                     International Association of Jewish Genealogical Societies
                     (IAJGS)
                     P.O. Box 251683, West Bloomfield, MI 48325-1683, USA

Via E-mail: Send an e-mail message to:
                     jajgsaddr@jewishgen.org
                     (an automated message processor).

Via WWW: On the World Wide Web (WWW), look at the URL.
                     http://www.jewishgen.org/iajgs/iajgs-jgss.html

In Print: The addresses of all Jewish Genealogical Societies are published
                     annually in the Spring issue of AVOTAYNU (PO Box 99,
                     Bergenfield, NJ 07621, U.S.A.

Additional Reading

Avotaynu, the International Review of Jewish Genealogy
published by Avotaynu Inc., 155 N. Washington Avenue,
Bergenfield, N.J. 07621-1742, U.S.A.
Tel: 201 387 7200 - Fax: 201 387 2855
E-mail: info@avotaynu.com.
Web-site: http://www.avotaynu.com

Weiner, M.   Jewish Roots in Poland, Miriam Weiner Routes to Roots
                   Foundation/YIVO, 1997

Weiner, M.   Jewish Roots in Ukraine and Moldavia, Miriam Weiner Routes to
                   Roots Foundation/YIVO, 1999

Wynne, S.   Finding your Jewish Roots in Galicia. Avotaynu, 1998

International Special Interest Group (SIG) Journals - Gesher, Galicia and Etsi.
(Details from the JGSGB). There are a number of others e.g. Stammbaum
(German SIG), Latvian SIG, Belarus SIG and Southern African SIG.

GENEALOGY BIBLIOGRAPHY FOR THE U.K.
Cyril Fox

GENERAL

Cox, J.	New to Kew?
Hartfield, E.	A Commercial Directory of the Jews of the UK 1894
Mordy, I.	My Ancestors were Jewish. How can I find out more about them? Soc. of Genealogists. 1995 (available from Family Record Office)
Samuel, E.	Jewish Births, Marriages & Deaths. In The National Index of Parish Registers: Vol. 3 Soc. of Genealogists 1974 pp 961-75
Samuel, W.	Sources of Anglo-Jewish Genealogy. London. Jewish Museum Pub. No.2 1933

Also

Many useful articles are in Transactions of The Jewish Historical Society of England (J.H.S.E). - a complete set is available in The Jewish Genealogical Society of Great Britain's (JGSGB) Library with index.

TOWNS & JEWS

CAMBRIDGE UNIVERSITY LIBRARY

Benas, B.L.	Records of the Jews in Liverpool: a paper. 1900
Buckman, J.	Immigrants and the Class Struggle: The Jewish Immigrant in Leeds 1880-1914. 1983 *
Freedman, M.	1891 Census, Leeds: List of Jewish Residents/ Extracted, Compiled and Computed by Murray Freedman 1994
Freedman, M.	Leeds Jewry: The First Hundred Years. 1992*

| Harris, P. | Israel at Forty: The Manchester Connection. 1988 |

* These books are also available at the British Library

BRITISH LIBRARY

Birmingham
| Josephs, Z. | Birmingham Jewry 1749-1914.   1980 |
| Josephs, Z. | Birmingham Jewry   More aspects 1740-1930 1984 |

Glasgow
Collins, K.E.	Glasgow Jewry: A Guide to the History and Community of the Jews in Glasgow. 1993
Collins, K.E.	Second City Jewry: The Jews of Glasgow in the Age of Expansion, 1790-1919
Levy, A.	The Origins of Glasgow Jewry, 1812-1895. 1949

Leeds
| Freedman, M. | Leeds Jewry: The First Hundred Years. 1992 |

London
Alderman, G.	London Jewry and London Politics 1889-1986 1989
Kosmin, B.A.	The Social Demography of Redbridge Jewry. 1979
Levy, C. & Wigodsky, P.	The Condition of East End Jewry in 1888. 1986
White, J.	Life in an East End Tenement Block 1887 -1920 1980

Manchester
| Dobkin, M. | Tales of Manchester Jewry and Manchester in the Thirties. 1986 |
| Dobkin, M. | More Tales of Manchester Jewry. 1994 |

Williams, B.	The Making of Manchester Jewry 1740-1875. 1976
	They Came from the Haim: A History of Manchester Jewry from 1867 by Jewish Social Services (Greater Manchester). 1995

Portsmouth

Weinberg, A.	Portsmouth Jewry 1730's-1980's. 1986

Scotland

Collins, K.E.	Aspects of Scottish Jewry. 1987

Sheffield

Krausz, A.	Sheffield Jewry: Commentary on a Community. 1980

South Wales

Bimah: The Platform of South Wales Jewry. 1994

OTHER BOOKS (Towns & Jews) NB. All Jewish Historical Society of England (J.H.S.E). Transactions are in the JGSGB Library

Brighton

Spector, D.	The Jews of Brighton 1770-1900 J.H.S.E. Transactions XXII 1968-69

Bristol

Tobias, A. et al.	A Catalogue of the Burials in the Jewish Cemeteries of Bristol.

Canterbury

Births , Marriages & Deaths of the Canterbury Congregation 1830-1869 (Hyamson Collection - in the JGSGB Library)

Cornwall

Pearce, K. & Simmons, G.	The Lost Jews of Cornwall. 1999

Falmouth

Jacobs, A.	Jews of Falmouth. J.H.S.E. Transactions. XVII 1951-52

Gateshead

Levy, A.	Story of Gateshead Yeshiva. 1952
Olsover, L.	Jewish Communities of N.E,. England 1755-1980 1981

Ireland
Hyman, L.   The Jews of Ireland. J.H.S.E. 1972

Leeds
Kraus, E.   Leeds Jewry. 1964

Leicester
Levy, S.   Notes on the Jewry of Leicester. J.H.S.E.
                                 Transactions, V. 1902-05

Liverpool
Benas, B.   'A Survey of the Jewish Institutional History of
                                 Liverpool and District'.
                                 J.H.S.E. Transactions, XVII   1951-52

Ettinger, P.   Hope Place, Liverpool Jewry 1836-1930.   1930

Goldman, H.   Short History of the Allerton, Liverpool, Hebrew
                                 Congregation. 1965

London
Fishman, W.   The Streets of East London. 1979

Manchester
Williams, B.   The Making of Manchester Jewry. 1976

Portsmouth
Meisels, I.   The Jewish Congregation of Portsmouth 1766-
                                 1842. J.H.S.E. Transactions, VI   1908-10

Newman, E.   Portsmouth - Some New Facts about its Jewish
                                 Community'. J.H.S.E. Transactions, XVII   1951-52

Roth, C.   The Portsmouth Community and its Historical
                                 Background. J.H.S.E. Transactions, XIII   1932-35

Sheffield
Krausz, A.   Sheffield Jewry: Commentary on a Community 1980

South West England
Susser, B.   The Jews of South West England
                                 (Mostly about Plymouth)

Sunderland
Levy, A.   History of the Sunderland Jewish Community 1956

Twickenham
Finberg, H.F.   Jewish Residents in Twickenham in the Eighteenth
                                 Century. J.H.S.E. Transactions, XVI   1945-51

Scotland
Collins, K.   Aspects of Scottish Jewry

Wales
Henriques, U.   The Jews of South Wales. 1993

OCCUPATIONS

Naggar, B.   Jewish Pedlars & Hawkers 1740-1940
                                     (in the British Library)

Rubens, A.   Jews & the English Stage 1667-1850
                                     J.H.S.E. Transactions. XXVI. 1975

THE FOLLOWING BOOKS ARE ALL AVAILABLE IN THE JGSGB LIBRARY
(For a full list of books in the Society's library please see the JGSGB's web-site)

Baxter, A .   In Search of your European Roots. A Complete
                                     Guide to Tracing your Ancestors

Berger, D.   The Jewish Victorian. Genealogical Information from the
                                     Jewish Newspapers 1871-80. 1999

Black, G   The History of the Jews' Free School, London,
                                     since 1732. 1998

Blatt, W.   JewishGen FAQ - Frequently Asked Questions
                                     Pamphlet No. 12

Brown, V.   Celebrating the Family: Steps to Planning a
                                     Family Reunion

Cerny, J. & Elliott, W.   The Library. A Guide to the LDS (Mormon)
                                     Family History Library

Cox, J.   Tracing Your Ancestors in the Public Record Office

Gandy, M.   My Ancestor was Jewish, how I can find out
                                     more about him

Gibson & Peskett   Record Offices & How to Find Them

Greene & Fulford   To our Children's Children: Preserving Family
                                     Histories for Generations to Come

Guggenheimer , H.   Jewish Family Names and their Origins - an
                                     Etymological Dictionary

Lehman, R.   Laying out a Pedigree

McLaughlin, E.	Saint Catherine's House Interviewing Elderly Relatives Wills before 1858 Somerset House Wills from 1858 Do. The Census 1841-1881, Use and Interpretation
Markwell, F & Saul, P.	The Family Historian's "Enquire Within" (2nd. Edition)
Mordy, I.	My Ancestors were Jewish. How can I find out more about them? 1995
Pelling , G.	Beginning your Family History. (6th. Edition)
Rigal, G.	Marriages at the Liberal Jewish Synagogue 1912-1935
Stern, M.	Tracing Your Jewish Roots
Susser, B.	How to Read & Record a Jewish Tombstone
Susser, B	The Jews of South-West England. 1993
Torode, B.	The Hebrew Community of Cheltenham, Gloucester and Stroud. 1999
Tucker, C.	The Study of Jewish Family Names
Winner, A.	Draft of The Jewish Genealogical Society of Great Britain's Family Finder (Pamphlet No. 45)

NON-UK REFERENCE BOOKS

Beider, A.	A Dictionary of Jewish Surnames from the Russian Empire. Avotaynu Inc. Teaneck, NJ. 1993
Beider, A.	A Dictionary of Jewish Surnames from the Kingdom of Poland. Avotaynu Inc. Teaneck, NJ. 1996
Kurzweil, A.	From Generation to Generation Harper Collins, New York, 1994
Mokotoff, G. and Amdur Sack, S.	Where Once We Walked. A Guide to Jewish Communities Destroyed in the Holocaust. Avotaynu Inc. Teaneck, NJ. 1991
Zubatsky, D.S. and Berent, I.M.	Source Book for Jewish Genealogies and Family Histories. Avotaynu Inc. Teaneck, NJ. 1996

RESOURCES AVAILABLE FROM SHEMOT
Rosemary Wenzerul

ABOUT *SHEMOT*

Shemot is the Journal of The Jewish Genealogical Society of Great Britain.

It is published quarterly and is free to members of the Society. Individual copies of any issue of *Shemot* may be purchased from:

> The Jewish Genealogical Society of Great Britain
> PO Box 13288
> LONDON, N3 3WD.
>
> e-mail: jgsgb@ort.org
> website: www.ort.org/jgsgb

If you are trying to trace *Shemot* in a public library, it may help to quote the international reference number ISSN 0969-2258.

Shemot contains articles of a genealogical nature, which range from the personal experiences of an individual member including research methods and sources used to a short scholarly paper on a specific area of research. Areas of research cover mainly Eastern and Central Europe, the USA, Spain and Portugal, and of course Great Britain.

USEFUL ARTICLES

The JGSGB website contains a complete list of articles. The following resources are articles written in *Shemot* in connection with British research and may be of assistance in researching your families:

MONTH/YEAR	Vol	No	SUBJECT/AUTHOR
Winter 1992	1	1	First Steps in Jewish Genealogy in the UK
			Jewish Genealogical Societies Worldwide
			Indexing of London Synagogue Registers
			Genealogical Research into Government Records

MONTH/YEAR	Vol	No	SUBJECT/AUTHOR
Spring 1993	1	2	Greater London History Library
			Leeds Jewish Community
			Reading Hebrew Tombstones
			Sources for Tracing Family History
Summer 1993	**1**	**3**	**Parkes Library**
			Directory Enquiries
			The Society for the Jewish Family Heritage
			The Society Library - The Microfiche Collection
Autumn 1993	1	4	Computers in Genealogy
			Manchester Jewry - Guide for the Family Historian
			Cemetery Survey
January 1994	**2**	**1**	**Jewish Chronicle Naturalisation Lists**
			The Jews of Portsmouth - Sources and Information 1740-1870 by *Henry Roche*
May 1994	2	2	Clues Beyond the Grave by *Richard Gilbert*
July 1994	**2**	**3**	**History of Bristol's Jewry by *Judith Samuel***
June 1995	3	2	Beginning Genealogy by *Daniel Gleek*
			The Greater London Record Office by *Richard Gilbert*. Page 23 - Glossary
December 1995	**3**	**4**	**Computerisation of Genealogical Records by *Fred Weil***
April 1996	4	1	Historical Database of Scottish Jewry by *Harvey Kaplan*
			Spanish & Portuguese Sources by *Julian Kemper*
July 1996	**4**	**2**	**British Telecom Archives**
			Colindale Newspaper Library by *Rosemary Wenzerul*
			News about Jewish Gen
			Interpreting Symbols on Graves
			Some Useful General References
December 1996	4	4	Major New Database on World Wide Web by *Gary Mokotoff*
July 1997	**5**	**2**	**Willesden Cemetery History by *Rosemary Wenzerul***
October 1997	5	3	JGSGB Library Rules
			Scottish Jewish Archives
			British Telecom Archive move
			Jewish Names in Insurance Records by *George Rigal*
			Northampton's Jewish Perspective by *Michael Jolles*

MONTH/YEAR	Vol	No	SUBJECT/AUTHOR
December 1997	5	4	Cemetery Visit to Lauriston Road by *Rosemary Wenzerul*
			The Graveside of History by *David Jacobs*
March 1998	**6**	**1**	**Family Records Centre by *Rosemary Wenzerul***
June 1998	6	2	The Royal Geographical Society Map Room by *George Rigal*
			The AJEX Museum by *George Rigal*
September 1998	**6**	**3**	**The Jewish Cemeteries of East Kent by *Martyn C. Webster***
December 1998	6	4	Hyde Park Family History Centre by *Michele Anderson*
March 1999	**7**	**1**	**Document Care by *Bryan Diamond***
June 1999	7	2	Medical Records by *Rosemary Wenzerul*
			Tracing British Commonwealth Service Personnel WWI by *Harold Pollins*
			British Passenger Lists by *Debbie Beavis*
September 1999	**7**	**3**	**More Resources for Tracing WWI Service Personnel by *Harold Pollins***
December 1999	7	4	The Wiener Library by *Cyril Fox*
			Looking at Family Photographs by *Bryan Diamond*
			Photographing tombstones from *JewishGen (Internet)*

GLOSSARY OF YIDDISH TERMS
Cyril Fox

TRANSCRIPTION	ENGLISH	YIDDISH
ainikel	grandchild	אייניקל
aydem	son-in-law	איידעם
brit	circumcision	ברית
bruder	brother	ברודער
buba	grandmother	באבע
get	divorce	גט
kehilla	congregation	קהילה
ketubah	marriage contract	כתובה
chevre kadisha	burial society	חברה קדישא
chupah	wedding canopy	חופה
chussanah	wedding	חתונה
machatonim	in-laws	מחותנים
metzaveh	gravestone	מצבה
nudden	dowry	נדן
shneer	daughter-in-law	שנור
Shtetl	small market town	שטעטל
(very small ditto= shtetele; village =dorf)		
shul	synagogue	שיל שול
shvester	sister	שוועסטער
shvegerin	sister-in-law	שוועגערין
shvigger	mother-in-law	שוויגער
shvogger	brother-in-law	שוואגער
tochter	daughter	טאכטר
yerisha	inheritance	ורושה
yizkorbukh	yizkor (memorial) book of destroyed shtetl	יזכער בוך
zeen	son	זין
zeydah	grandfather	ציידע

Other Terms

landsman (pl: landsleit)   person from same town
landsmanshaft   association of people from same town
yichus   pedigree
mitzve   good deed

ABBREVIATIONS
Rosemary Wenzerul

FAMILY TREES

B	Birth
M	Marriage
D	Death
NK	Not known

CENSUS

H	Head of Household
WIFE	Wife
SON	Son
DAU	Daughter
UNM	Unmarried
MAR	Married
WID	Widower
SERV	Servant
DOM	Domestic

INSTITUTIONS

AJEX	Association of Jewish Ex-Service Men and Women
BOD	Board of Deputies
BT	British Telecom
FHC	Family History Centre (run by the Mormons - LDS)
FRC	Family Record Centre
GRO	General Register Office
HMSO	Her Majesty's Stationery Office
JMC	Jewish Memorial Council
LDS	Latter Day Saints (Mormons)
LMA	London Metropolitan Archives
ONS	Office of National Statistics
PCC	Prerogative Court of Canterbury
PCY	Principal Prerogative Court of York
PRO	Public Record Office
RAF	Royal Air Force
RGS	Royal Geographical Society

SYNAGOGUES

RSGB	Reform Synagogues of Great Britain
ULPS	Union of Liberal & Progressive Synagogues
US	United Synagogue

GENEALOGICAL

AJGS	Association of Jewish Genealogical Societies
AJHS	American Jewish Historical Society
AJHS	Australian Jewish Historical Society
FTJP	Family Tree of the Jewish People
IAJGS	International Association of Jewish Genealogical Societies
IGI	International Genealogical Index
JGFF	Jewish Genealogical Family Finder
JGS	Jewish Genealogical Society
JGSGB	Jewish Genealogical Society of Greater Boston
JGSGB	Jewish Genealogical Society of Great Britain
JHSE	Jewish Historical Society of England
SIG	Special Interest Group
SOG	Society of Genealogists

NEWSPAPERS/JOURNALS

©	Copyright
ISBN	International Serial Book Number
JC	Jewish Chronicle
LJN	London Jewish News
PP	Pages
PUB	Publication
TRANS	Transaction
VOL	Volume

COMPUTERS/INTERNET

CWGC	Commonwealth War Graves Commission
E-MAIL	Electronic Mail
ISP	Internet Service Provider
PC	Personal Computer
WP	Word Processor
WWW	World Wide Web

INDEX

E

F

G

H

I

J

NOTES

80